M000158202

Sun Signs Secrets

Sun Sign Secrets

Monte Farber & Amy Zerner

WEISERBOOKS
San Francisco, CA / Newburyport, MA

First published in 2014 by
Red Wheel/Weiser, LLC
665 Third Street, Suite 400
San Francisco, CA 94107
www.redwheelweiser.com

Sun Sign Secrets
The Complete Astrology Guide to Love, Work & Your Future

For information, address:

The Enchanted World of Amy Zerner & Monte Farber
Post Office Box 2299, East Hampton, NY 11937 USA
E-mail: info@TheEnchantedWorld.com
Website: www.TheEnchantedWorld.com

For information about custom editions, special sales,
premium and corporate purchases, please contact:

Red Wheel/Weiser, LLC at 978.465.0504 or info@redwheelweiser.com

Library of Congress Cataloging-in-Publication Data available on request

ISBN 978-1-57863-561-0

Design by Suzanne Albertson

Printed in the United States of America

EBM 10 9 8 7 6 5 4 3 2 1

For entertainment purposes only.

 Contents

✳ *Introduction* ✳

What's Your Sign?

When someone asks you "What's your sign?" you know what that person really means is "What's your astrological sign?" Professional astrologers more often use the phrase "Sun sign," a term reflecting the concept that a person's sign is determined by which of the twelve signs of the zodiac the Sun appeared to be passing through at the moment she was born, as viewed from the exact spot on Earth where she was born. The zodiac (from the Greek *kykylo zodiakos,* meaning "circle of animals") is the narrow band of sky circling the Earth's equator through which the Sun, the Moon, and the planets appear to move when viewed by us here on Earth.

Astrology's Gift

Astrology, which has been around for thousands of years, is the study of how planetary positions relate to earthly events and people. Its long and rich history has resulted in a wealth of philosophical and psychological wisdom, the basic concepts of which we are going to share with you in the pages of this book. As the Greek philosopher Heracleitus (c. 540–c. 480 BCE) said, "Character is destiny." Who you are—complete with all of your goals, tendencies, habits, virtues, and vices—will determine how you act and react, thereby creating your life's destiny. Like astrology itself, our Sun Sign Secrets is designed to help you to better know yourself and those you care about. You will then be better able to use your free will to shape your life to your liking.

Does Astrology Work?

Many people rightly question how astrology can divide humanity into twelve Sun signs and make predictions that can be correct for everyone of the same sign. The simple answer is that it cannot do that—that's newspaper astrology, entertaining but not the real thing. Rather, astrology can help you understand your strengths and weaknesses so that you can better accept yourself as you are and use your strengths to compensate for your weaknesses. Real astrology is designed to help you to become yourself fully.

Remember, virtually all the music in the history of Western music has been composed using variations of the same twelve notes. Similarly, the twelve Sun signs of astrology are basic themes rich with meaning that each of us expresses differently to create and respond to the unique opportunities and challenges of our life.

ARIES
March 21–April 19

ARIES
March 21–April 19

Planet: Mars
Element: Fire
Quality: Cardinal
Day: Tuesday
Season: spring
Colors: red (all shades)
Plants: red poppy, thistle, ginger
Perfume: frankincense
Gemstones: bloodstone, garnet, red jasper, fire opal
Metal: iron
Personal qualities: Honest, brave, and headstrong

Keywords

We call the following words "keywords" because they can help you unlock the core meaning of the astrological sign of Aries. Each keyword represents issues and ideas that are of supreme importance and prominence in the lives of people born with Aries as their Sun sign. You will usually find that every Aries embodies at least one of these keywords in the way she makes a living:

initiation • challenge • adventure • exploration • daring
courage • honesty • competition • innocence • action
aggression • energy • spontaneity • discovery • creativity

Aries' Symbolic Meaning

The first day of spring marks the beginning of the sign Aries, the symbol of which is the Ram. Each spring, the desire to mate and stake his claim to his territory drives the ram to display his fitness and bravery by butting heads with his competitors. After a few times, the one who can handle the headache and hasn't given up is the winner.

People born under the sign of Aries have a lot in common with their symbol, the Ram. They are willing to butt heads with those they think are standing in their way. Brave and headstrong, they approach matters directly and forcefully. They're always striving to get the job done quickly, and they hate deceit so much that they can sometimes be too honest for their own good.

Aries is the first sign of the zodiac, and Arians, as children of Aries are called, try to be the first in some way. They want to be independent and original. They don't like to be second or even to wait terribly long for anyone or anything, and this can make them seem impatient and aggressive if they don't get their way. They function best when they act on their first impulse and don't second-guess themselves. They value strength, survival, and the kind of vital, unstoppable nature that enables the early spring flowers to push their heads up through the hard wintered soil.

Aries is one of four Cardinal signs in the zodiac (the other three being Cancer, Libra, and Capricorn). The first day of each of these signs marks the change of season. This is why the Cardinal signs symbolize forward movement. People born during one of the Cardinal signs tend to be goal-oriented, active, enthusiastic, motivated, and ambitious individuals who initiate change and get things moving.

Aries is also one of three Fire signs (the other two being Leo and Sagittarius). People with lots of fire in their chart are active, spontaneous, enthusiastic, creative, self-sufficient, and romantic. This forceful Fire element can sometimes make an Aries too proud, bossy, or pushy, but such an individual is just expressing life's vitality and usually means no harm.

Arians often get into trouble for acting without any forethought or consideration of others. But their self-reliant personality helps them thrive when they are in charge or working alone. Their fiery, assertive, and courageous nature is always charming and charismatic.

Recognizing an Aries

People who exhibit the physical characteristics distinctive of the sign Aries have strong facial features, often with piercing eyes. Frequently dressing in original styles and bold colors, they know how to look their best. Their bodies are strong, and they walk with determination. Vital and energetic, they project an aura of pure sexiness.

Aries' Typical Behavior and Personality Traits

* willful and bossy
* daring
* moves forward, even if afraid
* direct, open, and honest
* gets things done quickly
* highly competitive, hating to lose
* self-assured
* adventurous and enterprising
* enthusiastic and optimistic
* possesses very clear goals
* likes to get her way

What Makes an Aries Tick?

More afraid of being afraid than of anything else, Arians are always trying to prove how brave they are. Arians must remember that fear and self-doubt are not signs of weakness or losing control; nor are they a guarantee of failure.

The "fight or flight" instinct is a basic characteristic of Arians. If an Aries feels even slightly afraid, the emotion makes him either lash out or panic. Rams must stay spontaneous and not let their fear cause self-defeating behavior or paralyze them into inaction and cause even more self-doubt.

The Aries Personality Expressed Positively

Aries who are driven to push the boundaries of their chosen passion display the self-reliant, confident, and resourceful personality of their sign. They realize that they are on their own, but that that is a good thing, as it motivates them to be a shining example of what it means to be your own person.

On a Positive Note

Aries displaying the positive characteristics associated with their sign also tend to be:

* action oriented, taking charge of situations
* energetic and enthusiastic
* inclined to engage in networking
* vivacious
* positive
* heroic
* guileless
* passionate

The Aries Personality Expressed Negatively

Aries who boss others around and seem to believe that they have no faults display the self-limiting tendencies of their sign. Their desire to get the job done well and quickly may cause them to treat others as lesser beings, especially those they fear may not be up to the task at hand. Aries need to be aware of their human frailties without thinking they are "bad" for having them.

Negative Traits

Aries displaying the negative characteristics associated with their sign also tend to be:

- jealous and intolerant
- recklessly impulsive
- bossy
- defiant
- immature
- insensitive
- thoughtless
- too honest
- quick to quit

Ask an Aries If...

Ask an Aries if you want to know how to achieve your goals. He'll tell you what you should be doing and how you should be doing it. Just remember that he'll also tell you if your goal is not achievable, so don't ask if you can't take hearing the honest truth. Knowing an Aries is like having your own military general on call, always ready, willing, and able to help you plan your campaign. Just make sure you're ready to work until you drop.

Aries As Friends

Arians make for fun and entertaining friends, but they are not usually interested in entertaining for its own sake; they usually have a reason for having a dinner party or gathering. They like to network and meet new people who might be interested in their work or ideas. Aries friendships don't last long if the other party doesn't understand that the Aries individual is highly competitive and focused on achievements and furthering her career.

Arians make friends with original thinkers, especially those wise enough to recognize their uniqueness. Arians are warm and giving when they feel understood, but can be snappish if they feel threatened or misunderstood. However, a person who will support an Aries friend can enjoy an enduring friendship.

Looking for Love

Arians like to make the first move, and they are usually not afraid to do so. Even if they are scared, they'll still make their move—and be quick about it. They won't wait for anyone or anything. Arians must be assertive in their relationships.

An Aries needs to be with someone who is as alive and ardent as he is, or so appreciative of his energetic approach to living that it makes the Aries flame burn even brighter. Arians want people to respond to them in a real and honest way, and they like to test people by seeing how they react to Arian directness. While Arians may seem disinterested and contradictory, they're just trying to determine who a person really is.

If rebuffed, an Aries will move on without another thought wasted on the person who rejected her. It's rare to find an Aries feeling the pangs of unrequited love.

Finding That Special Someone

An Aries looking for love is less like a pioneer and more like a prospector, and the rule in prospecting is "Gold is where you find it." Capable of meeting a potential romantic interest practically anywhere and everywhere, Arians are always alert and not at all shy when on the lookout.

First Dates

An ideal first date for an Aries would be one where the Aries is in charge. On the perfect romantic excursion, the Aries' date would go wherever the Aries wanted to go and would do exactly what the Aries wanted to do! Since

Arians like to be the first in everything, a movie premier, the opening of a new restaurant, or any place that has just opened would make a great setting for a night out. Arians like hot and spicy foods, so a Mexican or Indian restaurant would also be appropriate.

Aries in Love

The expression "All's fair in love and war" sums up Aries' approach perfectly. When it comes to love, Arians enjoy the chase and the challenge of overcoming obstacles as much as the conquest itself. They are not afraid to enter into a relationship with someone who is already involved with another person. Arians need an exciting partner who will never bore them—routine is the kiss of death for a love affair involving an Aries. Surprisingly, independent Aries needs more affection from a lover than any other sign in the zodiac.

Arians are attractive because of their natural energy. Excited by new challenges and experiences, Arians like to go on adventures with the one they love. They want their partner to be as interested and enthusiastic about their dreams and goals as they are.

Undying Love

Aries are less likely to settle down than people born under most signs. However, once they fall in love they do not second-guess themselves; they plunge in headfirst and give it their all. They like to be completely enmeshed in their partner's life. The evolved Aries does this because he wants to help his lover succeed, while the less-evolved Aries will try to control his partner as a way to reduce the fear that this lover may do the wrong thing. Anyone who wants a relationship with Aries to endure must let the Aries in. Everlasting passion is the hallmark of the long-term Aries relationship. Forever young, Arians work hard to balance the innocence of youth with the wisdom of years.

Expectations in Love

At all times and from all people, Aries expect honesty and passion. They also expect to be given the freedom to be themselves fully. But when in a loving relationship, this expectation becomes magnified tenfold, and nothing less than 100 percent of their lover's attention and devotion will do. Aries do not do well with partners who want to remain friends with former lovers. It's not that they're jealous; they simply expect that they will be all their lover needs and wants.

An Aries must be able to speak her mind forcefully, even if what she has to say is something that her partner or a prospective partner does not want to hear. She expects to be able to get angry and get over it quickly without her lover ever mentioning the experience again. Though highly aware of how strong and brave one must be to get by in life, Aries has a wonderful childlike quality and needs a lover with a sense of humor or who looks at things in a unique way.

What Aries Look For

Arians are looking for someone who is vibrant, positive, and authentic. They test everyone they're interested in, trying to find that special someone who is true to himself and not afraid of a strong partner—or anything else, for that matter. They'll endure both complexity and high drama to win a lover's affections, but once that battle is over, they will tolerate neither.

If Aries Only Knew...

If Aries only knew how brave they appear to be, they would never worry about having to put up an aggressive, overly confident front at the slightest feeling of self-doubt. Arians are so busy being their pure self that they don't realize that some consider them bossy. They don't crave power for its own sake; they simply are not comfortable when anything they are connected with is not clearly defined or resolved, and so they immediately take action to force all concerned to create a definite resolution.

Marriage

Aries wants a partner of whom she can be proud, yet a savvy partner would be wise to be modest about personal goals and to put effort into supporting those of the sensitive Aries. The person who becomes the spouse of a typical Aries must realize that the Aries will be quite happy to leave the day-to-day details to him but will want to be in control of all major decisions—starting with the wedding ceremony. Anyone who partners with an Aries can expect an exciting, stimulating, and creative relationship with plenty of affection and surprises. What's more, the Aries partner will always keep her word.

Aries' Opposite Sign

Libra, the Scales, is the opposite sign of Aries. Although relationships between Aries and Libra can sometimes be difficult, Libra can show Aries how to cooperate, share, and bring people together in harmony. Libra can intervene diplomatically, where Aries will charge in, forcibly making demands. Both signs are quite aggressive but for different reasons. Aries wants to get his way, while Libra wants peace and balance; both are willing to fight for what they believe.

Pairing Up

In general, if people display the characteristics typical of their sign, intimate relationships between an Aries and another individual can be described as follows:

Aries with Aries:	Harmonious, with occasional brief but spectacular arguments
Aries with Taurus:	Harmonious, as long as Aries is the boss
Aries with Gemini:	Harmonious and in constant motion

Aries with Cancer:	Difficult, because Aries has little patience for moodiness
Aries with Leo:	Harmonious, with great achievements possible
Aries with Virgo:	Turbulent in a romantic relationship, but good as friends
Aries with Libra:	Difficult, but common goals and enemies can make it work
Aries with Scorpio:	Turbulent and passionate in the extreme
Aries with Sagittarius:	Harmonious, with the kind of honesty only they can endure
Aries with Capricorn:	Difficult, because Aries feels restricted by Capricorn's dark side
Aries with Aquarius:	Harmonious in the extreme; a mutual admiration society
Aries with Pisces:	Harmonious if Pisces is willing to trust Aries to lead the way

If Things Don't Work Out

If Arians feel that they've been lied to or dishonored, there is the slightest of possibilities that they'll give a lover a second chance. However, if they've been humiliated, the relationship is over, and they never want to see the person who humiliated them again. Aries trust that they have the power to move on and start over. When an Aries has decided that she wants to go, there is no use trying to stop her.

Aries at Work

Aries do their jobs as if they own the company. This trait can manifest itself in several ways. Evolved Arians are willing to work until they drop to get the job done for the good of all. Others emulate the kind of owner who likes to have workers to boss around.

It is important that an Aries be able to work without too much interference or even supervision. Aries have the ability to work well with others, but they must be careful that they do not get distracted with the needs and goals of other people. They enjoy helping others to shine and can be content to share the glory with the group. But they mainly like to lead. Aries are goal oriented and will naturally formulate a plan for their own career advancement while immersed in the reality of their work. Aries are often impatient with the pace of others or with the speed at which they themselves are able to climb the ranks. However, they should avoid being too honest about that.

The innovative ideas of Aries are a rare commodity that must be valued and acted on immediately. Aries know they have something unique to contribute to any team, and if they are not allowed to do so, they will take their contribution elsewhere. Born explorers, they are interested in experiencing for themselves what is real, not simply accepting what other people say is real, and they will work tirelessly at anything they think is worth doing.

Typical Occupations

Aries like occupations where they can be free to exercise their creativity, imagination, and original approach to projects. They are great promoters and can accomplish a lot when faced with a short deadline. Publishing, publicity, advertising, and visual media production are natural professions for them to prevail in, as rapid decision making, a quick mind, and multiple skills are necessary attributes for these occupations.

Aries also excel as individual artists espousing a unique form of creative expression. They enjoy a job where initiative, intuition, inventiveness, energy, leadership qualities, and enthusiasm are required. The military, recruitment, training, and law enforcement are other fields that appeal to Aries. In a similar capacity, Aries make excellent surgeons and surgical nurses.

Aries are associated with positions that inspire activity in others. They gravitate to any position that has authority. Aries must be in command or they will lose interest. They work best at the beginning of a project, leaving the details and execution to other people.

Behavior and Abilities at Work

In the workplace, a typical Aries:

* displays contagious enthusiasm
* possesses the stamina to work long hours
* gets the job done early
* manifests loyalty and honesty
* takes an apolitical approach
* will quit if bored or unappreciated
* initiates ideas and concepts

Aries As Employer

A typical Aries boss:

* needs respect and loyalty
* calms down quickly if angered
* rewards hard work
* wants to see new, improved ways of doing things
* gets to the point quickly
* will do the job if subordinates fail to
* expects everyone to multitask

Aries As Employee

A typical Aries employee:

* looks for opportunities for advancement
* works best without close supervision
* can be careless with details and secrets
* comes up with original solutions

* isn't afraid of challenges or taking risks
* makes lists for herself and coworkers
* needs praise and other rewards

Aries As Coworker

Aries have the ability to anticipate what must be done and to do it without being told what to do. This makes them quite resistant to being directed by others. However, Aries will always be the first in line to volunteer. Aries have only two speeds, "off" and "on." When given the freedom to act on their instincts, they are willing to put their all into a project, even if it means working around the clock until the job is finished.

People who are insecure about their own capabilities may feel threatened by the display of Aries self-confidence, willpower, and ability. However, over time, when others see that the Aries' actions are not politically motivated, they will appreciate having such a dependable, uncompromising individualist on their team.

Details, Details

Aries prefers not to have to take care of the details of a job, but will do so if necessary. Aries would much rather make lists and help everyone get started, then hand the job off to someone they trust. They need to be able to take full credit for the successes and be able to explain away the failures of anything with which they are connected. Some astrologers feel that Arians have a problem finishing what they've started, but this only happens when the ability to get full credit gets taken away from them.

Money

Aries worry less about money than any other sign. They have no doubt that they'll be able to obtain enough money to get what they want. They seem blessed by fate with the ability to extricate themselves from financial problems using methods that others would overlook.

Many Arians are not comfortable with inherited wealth and may even work against their own interests by expending these resources faster than they can be replenished. They revel in any and all rewards that result from their own efforts or from ideas that are related to them personally. It is not unusual to find an Aries making money from an idea that arose from a personal experience or need, creatively translating it into something that can benefit both himself and others.

At Home

Arians always have several home improvement projects on their list. They must finish one before starting another or they will not finish any of them. They don't need much sleep, but they sleep well.

Behavior and Abilities at Home

Aries typically:

* gets annoyed easily if not permitted to "rule the roost"
* alternates between being totally busy and indulging in total relaxation
* dislikes feeling restricted
* spends money to make the home run smoothly
* will move if unable to feel secure at home for any reason

Leisure Interests

Aries like to show off their prowess and competitive nature on both the physical and mental planes. They enjoy competitive sports, hiking, and camping. They also enjoy playing cards and participating in other games and activities that give them the opportunity to win.

The typical Aries enjoys the following pastimes:

- hobbies that involve metal tools or cutting, such carpentry, quilting, or collage
- physical activities that are done alone (not team sports)
- competitions
- martial arts
- adventure vacations
- home renovations
- watching others do things that the Aries is good at

Arian Likes

- winning
- handmade items
- easy money
- new clothes
- red flowers
- spicy foods
- fast cars
- surprise parties
- instant gratification
- one-of-a-kind gifts

Arian Dislikes

- being late
- restrictions
- losing
- feeling hungry
- being bested unfairly
- standing in line

* indecision
* phonies
* plain food

The Secret Side of Aries

Inside anyone who has strong Aries influences is a sweet, innocent, childlike soul who wishes she didn't have to fight so hard to get things to be the way she knows they have to be. Aries' forceful nature conceals a basic vulnerability that needs praise and affection from trusted loved ones to counter the often harsh words and deeds of others who find themselves the object of Aries' willful acts.

Mars

The planet Mars rules the sign of Aries. Since ancient times, Mars has been thought of as "the angry red planet" and bears the name of the Roman god of war. Modern space explorations have revealed the planet to have a surface resembling one devastated by war.

But the fiery, hotheaded, quick-to-act image does not represent the complete astrological meaning of Mars. The planet represents willpower, the energy possessed by the ego that enables people to go after, gain, and accomplish what they want. Mars is how people assert themselves as individuals. Through Mars, one grows strong through challenge, competition, and debate and by being forced to confront the strength of personal desires and dedication. Mars rules the head and especially the face. He also rules weapons.

Like Mars, Aries is a "doer," a heroic inspiration to compatriots and a force to be reckoned with by the opposition. The energy of Mars helps Aries to accomplish goals without any personal compromise. If this energy is used for mindless, hostile aggression, Aries will quickly find that he is not the only one with strong desires.

Bringing Up a Young Aries

More than those born under almost any other sign, the Aries child needs to know that he is loved and valued. Despite the brave face Aries children put on, big hugs and constant reassurance are essential, especially after emotional bumps.

Young Arians must be helped to accept the fact that we all have limits and fears and that these, too, have a purpose—to keep us from doing things we should not be doing. If they are not successfully taught these lessons, there is the danger that fears will turn into phobias.

Aries youngsters will explore anything new to them in a cautious manner until they feel they understand it. Then they'll act as if they are experts and take risks inappropriate to their level of experience. Caregivers must continually expand the boundaries of what they're teaching an Aries child so there will be less of a tendency for the child to become a reckless know-it-all.

Simply saying "no" to an Aries child doesn't work, nor does persuasion or using other obedient kids as examples. Aries children of any age respond best to a challenge. Give an Aries child a test and he'll go into action, to prove he is better than anyone else—even if the test involves doing something he doesn't like.

The Aries Child

The typical Aries child:

* throws tantrums, but quickly recovers
* pays attention and wants attention
* has a competitive nature
* is capable of playing by himself
* displays a headstrong will
* studies in quick bursts

- has a loving and demonstrative nature
- is not afraid to do her own thing
- can have unusual phobias

Aries As a Parent

The typical Aries parent:

- plays like a kid
- gives a lot of appreciation and praise
- can create imaginative worlds
- can be abrupt and strict
- will raise children with good self-esteem
- may try to be controlling
- leaps to the defense of loved ones
- displays affection and generosity

Health

In astrology, Aries rules the head and the face. What's going on in an Aries' head—especially feelings of stress caused by fear of humiliation, missed deadlines, and lost opportunities—strongly influences what is going on in the body and makes Aries prone to headaches, toothaches, and unexplained neuralgia around the jaws. Arians can "burn out" from too much work. They're so busy, they haven't got time to be sick, but when they do fall ill, they make a speedy recovery. Aries need to be careful of doing things too quickly, as they may injure themselves with knives or scissors. They should take care not to strain their eyes. Little "time-outs" are good for an Aries: hot baths, five minutes in a hammock, a stroll in the fresh air—these will work wonders.

FAMOUS ARIES

Patricia Arquette

Johann Sebastian Bach

Alec Baldwin

Warren Beatty

Marlon Brando

Matthew Broderick

Charlie Chaplin

Joan Crawford

Russell Crowe

Leonardo da Vinci

Celine Dion

W.C. Fields

Al Green

Harry Houdini

Thomas Jefferson

Elton John

Eddie Murphy

Napoleon

Sarah Jessica Parker

Diana Ross

Gloria Steinem

Vincent van Gogh

Tennessee Williams

Reese Witherspoon

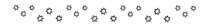

TAURUS
April 20–May 20

TAURUS
April 20–May 20

Planet: Venus

Element: Earth

Quality: Fixed

Day: Friday

Season: spring

Colors: spring green, blue, pink

Plants: daisy, magnolia, honeysuckle

Perfume: rose

Gemstones: moss agate, emerald, malachite, rose quartz

Metal: copper

Personal qualities: Loyal, pragmatic, good-humored, reliable, and musical

Keywords

We call the following words "keywords" because they can help you unlock the core meaning of the astrological sign of Taurus. Each keyword represents issues and ideas that are of supreme importance and prominence in the lives of people born with Taurus as their Sun sign. You will usually find that every Taurus embodies at least one of these keywords in the way he makes a living:

slow and steady • values money • nature • prosperity • caution control • security • tenacity • texture • beauty • habits • supplies kindness • calmness • romance • sensuality • sentimentality

harmony • food • organization • conservatism • hospitality
construction • working with minerals

Taurus' Symbolic Meaning

Taurus is one of the four Fixed signs of the zodiac (the other three being Scorpio, Aquarius, and Leo). Fixed signs are stubborn, stable, and resolute. And they have an understanding of the material world.

Taurus is also one of the three Earth signs (the other two being Virgo and Capricorn). The Earth signs are concerned with the physical world—what they can see, feel, hear, and touch. Earth is a symbol of the environment in which growth takes place. The Earth signs embody the concepts of nurture, security, and protection. They embrace moderation and conservatism.

Taureans get the earthly comforts they need by exerting their immense power in a sustained and methodical manner, no matter who or what tries to make them deviate from their routine. They function best when they are able to concentrate and stick to a plan, especially when they know their reward will be pleasure and luxury. Spontaneity can be a stretch, even a challenge for them. While they may not be the first to jump at a new idea, once they get started they will embrace it and follow it through to the finish. They are dependable and extremely loyal—to ideas, traditions, and the people in their life.

Recognizing a Taurus

People who exhibit the physical characteristics distinctive of the sign of Taurus have kind eyes, round faces, and good complexions. They have sturdy, muscular, and compact bodies, and sometimes have wide feet and short hands. They like to wear accessories around their necks, as well as comfortable clothing made of sensual fabrics and earthy colors. They tend to put on weight if they don't exercise regularly, and move slowly, with determination.

Taurus' Typical Behavior and Personality Traits

* is determined to succeed
* demonstrates shyness with new people
* copes well with difficult situations
* likes to sing
* is a deeply loyal friend
* possesses common sense
* likes good food and fine restaurants
* has a taste for luxury and beauty
* behaves in a pragmatic and stubborn manner
* works hard to build security
* assesses situations in financial terms
* is quiet and unpretentious
* can be wary and suspicious of others
* uses charm to get what he wants

What Makes a Taurus Tick?

Taureans value a middle-of-the-road approach to life. Not likely to get caught up in the latest trend, they believe in being themselves. Taureans need to understand that being true to their values does not mean they should be afraid to change their ideas or habits once in a while. They are not quick to engage in a confrontation, but swallowing too much anger can make them sick, literally and figuratively, or cause them to explode into a rage like a bull.

The Taurus Personality Expressed Positively

Taureans who are content with life radiate a glow of health and happiness. They are at their best when occupied with useful tasks that make their life and the lives of those around them more beautiful, harmonious, and fulfilling. Their ability to put events, both good and bad, into perspective allows them to see things practically, not emotionally.

On a Positive Note

Taureans displaying the positive characteristics associated with their sign also tend to be:

* patient and gentle
* attentive to aesthetics
* musically and artistically creative
* appreciative of the talents of others
* practical with resources
* good with plants and food
* demonstrative
* grounded and centered
* dependable with timing

The Taurus Personality Expressed Negatively

A Taurus who is either afraid of or uncomfortable with change displays one of the negative characteristics of the sign. Taureans may cling to traditional ideas more out of habit than principle. Even though this attitude may serve them well most of the time, it can also have a limiting effect on their progress and success.

Negative Traits

Taureans displaying the negative characteristics associated with their sign also tend to be:

* overly focused on material things
* too slow

- likely to stay in bad relationships too long
- possibly sloppy
- overly conservative
- embarrassed by free spirits
- skeptical
- self-indulgent

Ask a Taurus If...

Ask a Taurus if you want advice on how to increase your power and prestige. Taurus is never shy about giving tips and pointers, and will do it in such a nice way, you won't even realize you are being criticized. Thinking and planning in weeks instead of days, years instead of months, Taurus takes the long-term view of matters— and will expect you to do the same. The phrase "haste makes waste" expresses Taurus' viewpoint in a nutshell.

Taurus As Friends

Taureans make for gentle, charming, loving, and totally trustworthy friends. Because most Taurean individuals are unwilling to rely on others, they are usually very dependable themselves. A good Taurus will demonstrate a strong sense of loyalty to her friends. When it comes to friendship, Taurus looks for someone who is steady and devoted, and not given to panic or changes of plans. Those born under the sign of the Bull enjoy warm friendships with people who have good taste and with whom they can enjoy a good meal and converse about matters involving art, beauty, investments, and gardening. Highly affectionate toward their friends, Taureans enjoy calm, caring people who have the same qualities they do. The center of their universe is security, both physical and emotional, and through the gift of friendship they provide this treasure to others.

Looking for Love

Taureans enjoy simplicity. A Taurus will know he is in love when he just wants to be with a certain individual and watch that person live life naturally. Disliking signs of weakness, physical or emotional, a typical Taurus prizes a partner who has as strong a personality as he does. Taurus likes to share and savor power and resources. People who are rude, possess tacky taste, or have an unpleasant voice are unlikely to attract a Taurus.

Although Taureans are not usually picky, they do have certain standards. They don't like glib or shallow people, and it takes a great deal more than good looks and facile charm to turn their head. They enjoy compliments like anyone else, but they are much too level-headed to be taken in by them alone. Taureans are attracted to someone who is natural, plain-spoken, and sincere—someone who is not afraid to be herself.

Finding That Special Someone

To a Taurus, love is a natural, sensual, lusty experience that can be expected to last forever. A Taurus is attracted by physical beauty as well as by the successes and achievements of her partner. Romantic at heart, a Taurus is turned on by beautiful smells, flowers, colors, and music. Staying true to what she believes will improve a relationship greatly. When Taureans finally find their true love, they will achieve fulfillment.

First Dates

A good first date would be a concert or a football game, since Taurus loves music and enjoys any social, cultural, or sporting event. As far as choosing a restaurant is concerned, it is best if the Taurus picks the place or is consulted ahead of time, since those born under this sign are often excellent cooks and can be finicky about food. As Taureans can be reluctant conversationalists until they get to know a person better, they often won't share much personal information on a first date.

Taurus in Love

In love, Taurus has a slow, patient approach. It is important to Taurus that anyone he loves shares his personal tastes and desires. Taureans delight in deluxe comfort. So, for instance, although they love nature, they do not like to camp out. If a partner doesn't possess a similar love of comfort, there will eventually be a parting of the ways. When in love, Taureans are kind and gentle. They are natural and earthy in bed, and have a healthy self-image when it comes to their own body.

Undying Love

A Taurus can feel hurt and let down when she realizes that her partner is a human being with many faults. But a Taurus can also feel that she has to give the appearance of being blindly devoted to her partner, or to maintain some other kind of false personality, if the relationship is not going well. What Taurus really needs is a situation where each person loves the other for his or her true self; Taureans don't do well in relationships where each individual is trying to change the other. Taurus needs to seek a relationship that is a union of two independent people who are secure in as many ways as possible. Being with someone not because of who they are but because of what that person can offer will not lead to happiness.

Expectations in Love

Taureans believe in setting high standards, especially at the beginning of a relationship. Their fundamental concern is that their love be grounded in reality, and that they not become involved in some sort of superficial infatuation that won't last. Because they have generally realistic expectations about romance, Taureans are seldom disappointed in love. They are not likely to be drawn into a relationship that is based solely on lust and good times, nor do they expect any love affair that begins on that note to grow into something deeper and more significant.

For Taurus, loyalty is paramount in a relationship. They expect their ideas, desires, and dreams to be applauded and supported. They also like to receive sincere compliments on their appearance and accomplishments.

What Taurus Looks For

Taureans require harmony with a partner. While they don't expect to be agreed with at every turn, they want the sort of relationship where any sort of dispute is handled with respect and good humor. Taureans can have their head turned by good looks, but only if the person they are attracted to has an equally beautiful spirit. They appreciate intelligence but are not likely to be attracted to someone who shows off their knowledge.

If Taurus Only Knew...

If Taureans only knew that their homespun wisdom was held in such high esteem by the individuals who deal with them, they would stop secretly wondering if others find them interesting. While Taureans are comfortable with their communication skills, they may not feel that they are as witty and wise as other people. They need to realize that it is the strength and sincerity of their speech that makes the emotions they convey so believable and endearing.

Marriage

Taureans are stable, commonsense people who value home and family. While they make devoted partners, they can also be deeply possessive. Taureans like to be appreciated, and they believe in expensive gifts. No partner can force a Taurus into making a decision without allowing time for thought and consideration. That said, Taureans are highly capable and have an instinctive understanding of what to do in important situations. Partial to creature comforts, they like their home to be elegant and beautiful. Not surprisingly, Bulls are often bullheaded about their opinions, which can sometimes lead to incidences of emotional bullying, although these are rare. Sexually, they are intense, yet gentle.

Taurus' Opposite Sign

Scorpio is the opposite sign of Taurus. Because both signs are stubborn, relations between the two can be difficult. However, Scorpio can show a Taurus how to gain insight into the needs and motives of other people, and ultimately into the Taurus' own life. While Scorpio's intensity and drive mirror Taurus' determination, the Bull can learn a great deal about the spiritual terrain of love and commitment from Scorpio. Like Taurus, Scorpio is slow to forgive.

Pairing Up

In general, if people display the characteristics typical of their sign, intimate relationships between a Taurus and another individual can be described as follows:

Taurus with Taurus:	Harmonious, but can sometimes be lacking in excitement
Taurus with Gemini:	Harmonious, despite considerable differences in personality
Taurus with Cancer:	Harmonious because Taurus understands Cancer's sensitivity
Taurus with Leo:	Difficult, with arguments about money being a constant factor
Taurus with Virgo:	Harmonious in the extreme—a very tender love story
Taurus with Libra:	Turbulent yet affectionate and passionate

Taurus with Scorpio:	Difficult in the extreme, with periods of obsessive passion
Taurus with Sagittarius:	Turbulent if Taurus attempts to make Sagittarius conform
Taurus with Capricorn:	Harmonious, due to comparable values and goals
Taurus with Aquarius:	Difficult, but a sense of humor is a big help
Taurus with Pisces:	Harmonious, with both partners supporting each other's dreams
Taurus with Aries:	Harmonious, but requiring a respect for boundaries

If Things Don't Work Out

When Taureans are comfortable in a romantic relationship, it can be difficult for them to deal with the idea of changing the status quo, even when the relationship is not working. As a result, they tend to keep their unhappiness and disappointment bottled up inside, hoping that things will get better. However, once they come to understand that the only way to reclaim their own power is by leaving the relationship gone bad, they will do so without wringing their hands over the consequences.

Taurus at Work

Never flashy or dramatic, Taureans believe in getting the job accomplished through hard work and dedicated persistence. It is not necessary or even important for them to receive accolades for their performance in the workplace. Just knowing that they are doing a good job and earning their paycheck is enough for them.

The congenial personality that Taureans tend to possess is a big plus in the workplace. Reliable, unflappable, and graced with a professional attitude, they make excellent personal assistants. No matter how many tasks they are expected to finish in a given day, they never appear to be overwhelmed. Because of their discretion, they can be counted on to keep the confidences entrusted to them by an employer. They are not likely to gossip or get involved in cliques.

Even though they are independent minded and set in their ways, Taureans make excellent team players because they never put anything above getting the job done. While it can be hard at first to convince them to handle a task in a way that is foreign to them, they will gladly fall into line once they have been made to understand that this method will improve chances for accomplishing a goal in a way that benefits everyone concerned.

Typical Occupations

Taureans do well in banking and finance, transportation, construction, conservation, landscaping, farming, engineering, and mathematics. The sign is also associated with floristry, food, general medical practice, executive secretarial positions, stable occupations in established institutions, and any type of job that involves land, investments, minerals, or other hard goods. They have a natural affinity for working with their hands. Careers that help to make someone's environment more beautiful and harmonious are particularly relevant to them.

Thoroughness and single-mindedness that can become dogmatic are well-known traits of the persistent Taurus personality. No detail will ever be overlooked. Interior design, architecture, and the fine arts—especially sculpture, fashion, music, and singing—are also good fields for Bulls. Often graced with pleasant speaking voices, they do well in sales or any work that requires a lot of oratory.

Behavior and Abilities at Work

In the workplace, a typical Taurus:

* values tradition
* hates to be interrupted
* demonstrates a steady and reliable work ethic
* requires a routine and a plan
* stays on schedule
* does not give up
* needs clear goals

Taurus As Employer

A typical Taurus boss:

* is a good judge of character
* works to increase income for the company
* looks for loyalty and honesty
* does not make hasty decisions
* expects to be respected
* won't budge if pushed
* cannot be manipulated

Taurus As Employee

A typical Taurus employee:

* doesn't like freelance jobs
* behaves honestly
* deals with matters in a down-to-earth and sensible way
* demonstrates punctuality
* will rarely be pushed to anger
* excels when it comes to dealing with numbers

Taurus As Coworker

Taureans believe in compartmentalizing their lives, so they are just as unlikely to bring work problems home as they are to discuss personal matters at work. Although friendly and pleasant, they seldom develop deep friendships with coworkers.

Details, Details

Taureans can appreciate the saying "God is in the details" more than those born under almost any other sign. While they can appear to work in a slow, even plodding way, Taureans believe that it is better to take a little longer to accomplish a chore than to speed through a task and make mistakes.

Some signs may find details boring, but Taurus never does. In fact, it is in details that he is able to see the overall significance of a project. Taurus possesses a natural ability to work with figures. The Bull is much better at acting as a facilitator of someone else's ideas than at being the "idea person" behind a project. They will not feel insulted or demoted in any way if they are assigned work that is largely detail oriented, rather than creative in nature.

Taureans will seldom miss a day of work. This is a result of not only loyalty and good habits, but also the understanding that the best work is accomplished over the long haul. Taurus' self-esteem improves when he feels good about the job he does.

Money

Extremely risk averse, Taurus is not the type for gambling of any sort. Yet, motivated by a desire to obtain and accumulate material possessions, Taureans can be compulsive in their intensity to secure an ample supply of the things they consider important to their comfort and happiness. Worrying about money can be highly stressful for them, so they should not attempt to stretch their resources to the limit. Taureans should put money in safe and secure investments such as a savings account or IRA, rather than attempt to be a financial wizard. Existing financial resources should be properly allocated, used, and developed. Some Taureans will envy the resources of their richer friends or family members, but most appreciate the wisdom of being satisfied with the good things they already possess.

At Home

For Taureans, home is a place to feel absolutely secure. Beauty is an important component of their surroundings, but comfort is an even more valuable asset. Cooking, cleaning, and working in the garden are more appealing to most Taureans than engaging in social activities.

Behavior and Abilities at Home

Taurus typically:

* enjoys do-it-yourself repairs
* is adept at planning nutritious menus
* runs a well-organized home
* likes to be in charge of decorating projects
* believes that harmony is expressed through color

Leisure Interests

Beautifying the home, office, and backyard, or going to a concert, play, art exhibit, or any other cultural event are activities that Taureans are likely to enjoy, as long as they are able to relax, take their time, and savor the beauty and creativity of the experience. At home, Bulls like to settle back on a nice cozy couch, listening to their favorite music or watching a romantic DVD.

The typical Taurus enjoys the following pastimes:

* expanding a music collection
* craft and art projects
* home improvement projects
* working with plants and flowers
* counting money
* taking naps

Taurean Likes

* jewelry
* sculpture
* gardens
* sensual colors and shapes
* a regular routine
* a wonderful meal
* attractive surroundings
* expensive birthday presents
* vacations
* chocolate

The Secret Side of Taurus

Taureans love the best things in life, and long to be rich, retired, and surrounded by beauty. But they secretly fear that they won't have enough material resources to make their dreams come true. Those born under this sign like to appear cool, calm, and collected. But when they do eventually express anger, it can be devastating to those around them and so disturbing to themselves that it takes a while for them to recover both their composure and their self-esteem.

Venus

Venus—known in astrology as the planet of love, affection, values, and sensuality—rules the sign of Taurus. Sociable Venus also rules over parties and pleasurable meetings. She accomplishes her goals by attracting only what she wants and rejecting the rest, thus making taste and values two of her special talents. The love and beauty of Venus have the power to both unite and heal us. Venus also rules our senses of touch, taste, and smell.

Like Venus, Taurus can be highly affectionate and fond of the good life, as long as it is a peaceful, secure existence. Taureans rarely deviate from their personal code of what is right, even in the search for pleasure. Those whose birth charts have a strong Taurus influence tend to possess a firm set of personal values.

Bringing Up a Young Taurus

Young Taurean children respond to practical direction and common sense. They don't like to be pushed or forced, but instead tend to listen and respond to calm and gentle direction, especially if it is delivered with patience and a soft tone of voice. Generally well behaved and sweet tempered, Taurean children can also be highly stubborn and will dig in their heels when confronted with new challenges, such as sharing with other children. Take your time with Taurean youngsters, as the slow-and-steady approach works best. In dealings with them, stressing routine and sticking with established goals are advantageous.

Physical affection is essential to the healthy growth of any Taurean child. Young Taurus also needs a harmonious environment in which to flourish. Colors, sounds, and smells will affect these children quite deeply. Surrounding them with shades of spring green, light blue, pink, and rose, as well as soft music, provides reassurance and comfort.

It is good to teach Taurean children about the importance of ethics and commitment. Teaching by example is crucial and will result in their learning important lessons that they can take into their teen years and adulthood.

The Taurus Child

The typical Taurus child:

- responds to comfort and affection
- is generally good-natured
- may excel in singing or other forms of music
- possesses more strength than one would suspect
- is usually cuddly, calm, and affectionate
- can be obstinate
- may dislike scratchy or woolen clothes
- may be prone to sore throats
- usually works slowly but steadily at school
- may be selfish with toys or other possessions
- should be encouraged to play sports
- is likely to have many friends

Taurus As a Parent

The typical Taurus parent:

- is judicious in dispensing discipline
- encourages music lessons
- believes in taking children to cultural events
- teaches the importance of good grooming
- enjoys singing to her child
- encourages his child to have friends
- creates an atmosphere of harmony at home

Health

Taureans usually enjoy good health throughout their lives, but when they do experience issues, the problems tend to occur in the sinus area, throat, and lungs. These parts of the body can be subject to repeated infections. Neck and voice problems are also common complaints, as the body part that Taurus rules is the neck.

Taureans tend to like sweet desserts, which, eaten frequently or in abundance, can eventually lead to weight issues. Fatty, high-calorie cuisine should be avoided. Taureans should also stay away from foods that are high in sodium or caffeine, as these can have a troublesome effect on their systems. To maintain their health, Bulls should exercise regularly, and, in particular, should take long walks. Taurus loves the outdoors, so meditative time spent in gardens and fresh air would be a healthy habit to develop.

FAMOUS TAUREANS

David Beckham

Candice Bergen

Pierce Brosnan

James Brown

Carol Burnett

Catherine the Great

Cher

Kelly Clarkson

Penelope Cruz

Salvador Dalí

Tony Danza

Queen Elizabeth II

Sigmund Freud

Audrey Hepburn

Jay Leno

Shirley MacLaine

Tim McGraw

Willie Nelson

Jack Nicholson

Al Pacino

Michelle Pfeiffer

William Shakespeare

Barbra Streisand

Uma Thurman

Orson Welles

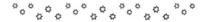

GEMINI
May 21–June 20

GEMINI
May 21–June 20

Planet: Mercury

Element: Air

Quality: Mutable

Day: Wednesday

Season: summer

Colors: white, yellow

Plants: sweet pea, lily of the valley, mint

Perfume: lavender

Gemstones: quartz crystal, tiger's eye, topaz, bicolored tourmaline

Metal: quicksilver

Personal qualities: Witty, changeable, versatile, talkative, well read

Keywords

We call the following words "keywords" because they can help you unlock the core meaning of the astrological sign of Gemini. Each keyword represents issues and ideas that are of supreme importance and prominence in the lives of people born with Gemini as their Sun sign. You will usually find that every Gemini embodies at least one of these keywords in the way she makes a living:

> *haste • logic • social skills • communication • mischief*
> *restlessness • gossip • versatility • curiosity • precocity*
> *life of the mind • rumor mill • advertising • quick wit*

talkative • salesmanship • travel • the media • adaptability
numbers • estimate • sound bites • information

Gemini's Symbolic Meaning

Thousands of years ago, the ancient sages were wise to pick as the symbol for Gemini a pair of twins. For it is as if there exist within the Gemini two different people with two different sets of values and opinions. Personifying this concept of duality, Geminis are known for functioning best when they have two or more things to do at the same time.

Those born under the sign of the Twins are among the best communicators of information, in terms of both relaying what they've learned and expressing their opinions. However, though they speak clearly, their tendency to use big words and long sentences often results in others having difficulty understanding the precise nature of what Geminis are trying to say.

Interested in everything, Geminis become skilled at anything they put their lightning-quick minds to. They are also the most versatile of signs: It is rare for a Gemini to do only one thing extremely well. Additionally, those born under this sign have great mental dexterity. Their desire to comprehend and communicate quickly produces both an endless curiosity and an ability to take every side of an issue.

Gemini is one of the four Mutable, or changeable, signs of the zodiac. (The other three are Sagittarius, Pisces, and Virgo.) Mutable signs are flexible and variable—they know how to adapt and adjust. Geminis are curious to know everything there is to know, and they are more than willing to adjust their beliefs when information that appeals to them comes along. All Mutable signs possess a talent for duality, but because Gemini is the sign of the Twins, this trait is strongest in them.

Gemini has an abundance of intellectual energy, which ties in to its being one of the three Air signs (the other two are Aquarius and Libra). Air signs have in common the desire for communication and freedom of expression, thought, and movement. Air is a metaphor for the invisible thoughts and ideas that motivate Gemini.

Geminis love to gossip. While most don't engage in this activity more than other people, they are better at it and delight in it more. You can bet that when a Gemini tells you something, it is the most up-to-date information available. Geminis love to be up on the latest things, and they try their best to know something about everything. Their curiosity is legendary. Geminis think that if they only had the time and access to enough information, they could actually come to know *everything*.

Recognizing a Gemini

Geminis can be tall and usually have long arms and legs. While highly agile and light on their feet, they can be somewhat clumsy when hurrying. Possessing a great deal of nervous energy, they find it difficult to sit still, and they tend to use their hands to express themselves. They generally smile and laugh a lot, and have a knack for looking younger than they really are.

Gemini's Typical Behavior and Personality Traits

- friendly and outgoing
- intelligent and witty
- graced with superior social skills
- expert at telling jokes and stories
- gives useful advice
- optimistic and upbeat
- takes an interest in friends' interests
- loves to read
- curious about many subjects
- adept at multitasking
- may change his mind often

What Makes a Gemini Tick?

Geminis want to experience life fully and in as many different ways as they can. They may even go so far as to live something of a double life. At the very least, they have two opinions about everything—more, if they have actually studied a particular subject in depth. Geminis hunger for information from all sources: books, television, word of mouth. They will do practically anything to avoid being bored—which, to a Gemini, is a fate almost worse than death.

The Gemini Personality Expressed Positively

Geminis who are interested in everything are expressing the best qualities of their sign: versatility, dexterity, and intelligence. When Geminis are happy they are a joy to be around, displaying their intelligence in a witty way that isn't snobbish or vain. And they delight in being able to help anyone who is not as quick-witted, knowledgeable, or versatile as they are.

On a Positive Note

Geminis displaying the positive characteristics associated with their sign also tend to be:

* articulate and entertaining
* adaptable and versatile
* open to alternative ways of thinking
* good with their hands
* youthful in attitude and appearance
* witty and charming
* inquisitive and smart
* graced with a quick mind and body

The Gemini Personality Expressed Negatively

Few people who see the lighthearted and upbeat side of Gemini ever suspect that the very same person can often feel desperately alone and lost. This is usually caused by the Gemini's tendency to distance herself from her feelings and examine them as if they belong to someone else. If a Gemini doesn't have a way to channel her love and need for communication, there is a tendency to turn sarcastic and critical.

Negative Traits

Geminis displaying the negative characteristics associated with their sign also tend to be:

* prone to boredom
* often nervous and restless
* fickle and unreliable
* impatient and irritable
* impractical with money
* gossipy and likely to tell fibs
* quick to size people up
* untrue to their word

Ask a Gemini If...

Ask a Gemini if you want to know how to get to a specific location. Those born under the sign of the Twins have a flawless sense of direction and will probably also treat you to a history of the place, as well as other background information. You can also depend on them for the details of what is going on in the world, because no matter how demanding their schedules may be, Geminis always manage to read the paper or catch the news on television or online.

Geminis As Friends

Geminis make for spirited, fun friends who are eager to try new adventures. Drawn to lively, intelligent conversations, they like people who share their curiosity about the world. They generally enjoy spending time with individuals who respond well to or enjoy spontaneous activities and spur-of-the-moment plans. Geminis never want to miss anything, and hence may end up being early or late for a get-together. They love to network and are not at all possessive when it comes to sharing their contacts.

Geminis will keep friends amused with endless observations, stories, bits of information, or the latest gossip. Often the friendships won't last long because the restless and fickle Gemini nature gets bored quickly and thus is always ready to move on, meet new people, and make new friends.

Looking for Love

Geminis may sometimes find that they are interested in more than one person, even if they are in a committed relationship. It is also possible that more than one person may be interested in *them*. There can be quite a difference in age, station in life, or educational background between a Gemini and her partner(s), because those born under the sign of the Twins see variety as the spice of life, something to be savored and enjoyed. Rather than look for carbon copies of themselves, Geminis are challenged and excited by intellectual, emotional, and spiritual differences. Because of their adaptable nature, they find it easy to embrace the interests and hobbies of others.

Reading, writing, learning, and growing must be an important part of any new relationship a Gemini enters. Taking courses or developing skills together can improve the chances of love blossoming. For a Gemini, the promise of an intellectual partnership may be what is most attractive in another individual. It is practically impossible for Geminis to be romantic with someone with whom they can't communicate.

Jealousy may enter the picture because the Gemini is not home or is paying a lot of attention to others around him. This may appear to be flightiness, but it is a way of being honest to the sign's nature. Geminis like to relate to many people at the same time—otherwise, they might get bored. It can be difficult for Geminis to make peace with the idea that one person can satisfy all of their needs. But even if they can come to grips with the concept of sexual fidelity, the typical Gemini may still have to go to one or more other partners for intellectual or emotional stimulation.

Finding That Special Someone

Geminis love to flirt, and it can be difficult to spot someone special amongst their many crushes. Finding a special someone frightens Geminis out of superficiality, and they must avoid becoming overly serious and obsessive in their effort to keep this special person around. Geminis need stimulating communication. They are likely to meet romantic partners in places where they can feel secure, such as in Internet chat rooms, bookstores, libraries, and museums. Anything related to learning and scholarship, including debates, will put them in the mood.

First Dates

The perfect first date should take place in a conversation-friendly zone. Given Gemini's love of being up on the latest and greatest, a unique or trendy restaurant makes for an appropriate setting. Food isn't really a Gemini "thing," but when it comes to eateries, ambience matters a great deal. Going to the movies, especially to see a comedy, is always a great first date for Gemini, so long as there is the opportunity to go somewhere afterward and talk about it. The same holds true for a motivational lecture, seminar, play, or other cultural activity.

Gemini in Love

Geminis seek variety in love and enjoy surprises and lighthearted romance. Geminis want friendship, warmth, and shared ideas. They enjoy humor in a relationship, but they prize communication. They have great instincts about people and rarely jump into a relationship without first understanding what the results are likely to be. Their mental gyrations can be exhausting, and they sometimes fear the fact that there are at least two distinct people inside of them. Their partner must be comfortable with this and, ideally, loves them for it.

Undying Love

Geminis can be cynics, so when they find a soul mate, they are both elated and amazed. Geminis are smart and worldly, but thinking about the latest facts and the perfect comeback line can keep them from hearing their heart speak to them. Geminis need to understand that love is one area of life where analytical intelligence isn't a help. In fact, it can be something of a hindrance.

Geminis don't expect to be disappointed in love, but rather they find it hard to believe that such a perfect understanding can exist between two people.

Expectations in Love

Communication excites Geminis, while silence and detachment turn them off. They interpret silence as a form of opposition and feel that they are being ignored. Geminis do not have just two or three opinions to express; it is as though they are two or three different people, and this characteristic must be accepted by those who want to be close to them. Their change-ability can be annoying or interesting. The degree to which a Gemini is overwhelmed by confusing emotions will determine how warm or cool, or close or distant, he appears to be.

While Geminis feel emotions deeply, they find it difficult to express love. They need to see that their personal freedom and personal space are being respected. Knowing that they can become too emotionally dependent on another person worries them. They are very sensitive to their own hurt feelings. Choosing words carefully and making sure to be understood are very important in a relationship with a Gemini. Two people can hear the same words but interpret them in radically different ways.

What Geminis Look For

Geminis need to connect with other people, though they need not be nearby physically. Connecting to others through books, films, instructional videos, as well as through lectures and live performances, is what interests Geminis. They need the freedom to explore, investigate, and learn. Frequent opportunities to change direction, and follow several lines of interest at once, are essential. Geminis are not intellectual snobs and do not require a love interest who is highly educated—only someone who is curious about and excited by ideas.

If Geminis Only Knew

If Geminis only knew that it is just as easy to become the story as it is to repeat it, they would avoid gossip, even though it intrigues them. Stretching or elaborating the truth is not uncommon for Geminis, as they can hardly resist embellishing a story. Most people want to be known for their unwavering commitment to a bunch of opinions about what is true about life—most people other than Geminis, that is. With their remarkably adaptable nature, Geminis thrive on new ideas and opinions and are generally open to a change in perspective.

Marriage

Geminis will be drawn to a special someone who will stimulate them with brilliant concepts and ideas and who will enjoy people and friends as much as they do. They need a stimulating social life, so it is never wise for them to marry a wallflower.

The person who contemplates marrying a typical Gemini must realize that his mate has probably already had more than one partner and will not stay long with a person who is a stick-in-the-mud. Geminis are so mercurial that they need a partner who is willing to move, travel, and change plans often—or else the relationship won't work.

Geminis can be more high-strung than almost any other sign, but we like to say that you have to be high-strung to make great music together.

Gemini's Opposite Sign

Sagittarius is Gemini's opposite sign. Sagittarius can show Gemini how to look past her own Mercury-ruled fascination with details in order to see the broader view. Sagittarius has a great sense of humor, but unlike that of Gemini, it does not revolve around witty comments or wry observations. Sagittarius knows how to make fun of himself. Both signs are keen on education, conversation, and most of all, ideas. Like Gemini, Sagittarius needs a relationship that is based on far more than simply superficial attraction or sexual desire.

Pairing Up

In general, if people display the characteristics typical of their sign, intimate relationships between a Gemini and another individual can be described as follows:

Gemini with Gemini:	Harmonious, with amazing conversation as a highlight
Gemini with Cancer:	Harmonious, if Cancer is willing to listen to what Gemini has to say
Gemini with Leo:	Harmonious in public, less satisfying in private
Gemini with Virgo:	Difficult, because too many details dominate
Gemini with Libra:	Harmonious—a true mutual admiration filled with affection
Gemini with Scorpio:	Turbulent and emotional, but a real love match
Gemini with Sagittarius:	Difficult, but with a potential for teamwork

Gemini with Capricorn:	Turbulent, especially if values are different
Gemini with Aquarius:	Harmonious—a true meeting of the minds!
Gemini with Pisces:	Difficult, because Pisces wants to lean on Gemini
Gemini with Aries:	Harmonious, with special emphasis on passion and shared goals
Gemini with Taurus:	Harmonious, so long as there are shared goals

If Things Don't Work Out

Because she loves to be free without question, a Gemini does not feel comfortable with a partner who is harsh, jealous, or dominating. Confinement and boredom are the worst horrors to a Gemini; if a relationship ends, one or both of these elements is likely the culprit. There are rarely any bad feelings on Gemini's part—only a sense of wistfulness for what has been lost.

Gemini at Work

If a Gemini's work is boring or not challenging enough for his skill level, the best way for him to deal with it is to stay at his present job while planning and taking action to change jobs, or even careers. The time Geminis spend daydreaming about a new line of work might actually help them find a way to improve the experience of their *present* job—and they might even find that changing jobs is unnecessary. It might also be beneficial for Geminis to hold more than one job at a time. This will bring them into contact with more people who are in a position to help them.

A Gemini should let her desires be known in a way that conveys to others how they can benefit by helping the Gemini. The art of politics is first making the right connections and then using those connections skillfully.

If a Gemini's work is satisfying, then he may want to start branching out or taking on a second job. Holding two jobs might be easier and more beneficial than holding only one. The Gemini may want to go to school or take on-the-job training, since the chance to study something new is usually highly appealing to those born under the sign of the Twins.

Geminis' career goals or ambitions are rarely realized overnight. They would do best to try to accomplish many small successes over a period of time rather than one or two big ones that require too much pressure or ambition.

Typical Occupations

The best chance for a Gemini to attain success would be in writing, journalism, lecturing, touring, driving, local travel, or working with her hands. Geminis might be able to craft ways to use their everyday routines to their advantage: clever thinking may help them discover opportunities for improvement in ordinary aspects of modern life.

Working in sales is ideal for Geminis because of their abilities to persuade and talk about anything. No matter what profession Geminis enter, they should learn or craft new techniques to streamline their work and make sure that the path to their career goals is clear. They should take time to study as much as they can about their job and where they want to go with it in the future.

Behavior and Abilities at Work

In the workplace, a typical Gemini:

- is invariably an "idea" person
- is not always punctual
- can be a problem solver
- has creative ideas
- is well liked by colleagues

Gemini As Employer

A typical Gemini boss:

* is good at charming his employees
* is open to new ideas that will increase profits and cut costs
* makes changes to improve communications
* possesses an interest in the smallest details
* is approachable
* knows how every department works
* socializes with her employees

Gemini As Employee

A typical Gemini employee:

* likes a lot of activity
* enjoys running errands to get out of the routine
* likes to work on several projects at the same time
* can come up with a good idea quickly
* gets bored with bureaucratic red tape
* possesses an aptitude for multitasking

Gemini As Coworker

Geminis are good at small talk and office politics. They can keep a secret only if they can share it with at least one person, any person, anywhere in the world. Skilled at communication, they can help facilitate interactions between people who are not as good at expressing themselves. They enjoy being editors and fact checkers, and if you have a puzzle that needs solving, ask a Gemini. They are also fun, entertaining, and easy to work with.

Details, Details

Taking things a step at a time and paying attention to every detail are paramount to a Gemini's success. Making lists and establishing plans to accomplish goals in a logical order are very important to a Gemini. Details are not at all boring; rather, Geminis consider details the essence of their relationships with others as well as the embodiment of their job. This preoccupation with the particulars doesn't mean that a Gemini can't see the larger view of things. She understands that the larger picture is made up of a million little details.

Geminis see all sides of a situation, which can create the impression that they're not committed to anything. They may also appear to be nosey, while, in fact, they are simply collecting details of office life and occasionally talking about them. There is nothing malicious, though, in the way they talk about others.

Money

Building wealth is a game requiring discipline and the realization that small things matter. It would be helpful for a Gemini to learn all she can about accumulating and managing money—by reading books, taking courses, and so forth. Asking a successful relative for advice about how to attain and manage financial goals would also be beneficial. Then, whatever a Gemini learns should become a part of her everyday routine.

Investments related to communications, publishing, transportation, or education can benefit Geminis. Whatever they invest in, they should get out and see for themselves what the company really does and how it all works. Simply understanding an investment from an analytical point of view won't be enough.

At Home

As they are in the workplace, Geminis are perpetually in motion at home. They love having friends over for meals and are the most likely of all the twelve signs to work from their home.

Geminis hate the very possibility that they will be bored, so it is not uncommon to find them making several rooms in their home do double duty. Unlike most signs, they are quite happy to have their bedroom or kitchen be their office, their living room, or their game room; it keeps them from wasting time going from room to room.

Behavior and Abilities at Home

Gemini generally:

* likes a space that is light and cheery
* decorates with a variety of colors and interesting artwork
* needs a big bookcase
* likes to entertain
* enjoys making crafts for her home
* has lots of games to play

Leisure Interests

Typical Geminis like to listen to the television while they read, or have music on while they sing along and do the dishes. They need to be involved with a lot of activities to occupy their busy minds. They enjoy a good conversation or writing funny e-mails. Geminis often keep a diary, with some maintaining a continuous series of them dating back to childhood.

The typical Gemini enjoys the following pastimes:

* reading books and newspapers
* playing table tennis and billiards

- going bowling
- learning and using languages
- creating handmade gifts
- traveling short distances
- watching reality and variety shows
- taking short courses about new subjects
- testing interesting recipes

Gemini Likes

- telling a good story
- completing crossword puzzles
- doing several things at once
- planning trips
- talking on the phone
- heat-and-serve food or takeout
- being with friends
- novelty gifts
- gossip columns
- knowing a little about a lot of topics

Gemini Dislikes

- losing an argument
- waiting for an answer
- wasting time
- committing to a date
- inflexible people
- listening to complaints
- not knowing what's going on
- dealing with slow thinkers

* having to repress an opinion
* boredom and boring people

The Secret Side of Gemini

Because they are good at so many things, Geminis may give the impression of knowing everything. They are restless, and people who are just getting to know them may think that Geminis flit around from one passion to another too often. But it's not so much that Geminis change their mind a lot; rather, it's as though each Gemini individual is made up of several different people. By being of many minds at the same time, they remind us that there is not just a single way to look at a person or a problem.

Mercury

In Roman mythology Mercury is the messenger of the gods. The modern associations of the planet bearing the same name include all forms of communications, such as speech, writing, sign language, body language, facial expressions, and code. The planet also rules the means for such communications, such as writing implements, books, telephones, computers, wireless devices, pagers, televisions, satellites, and radios. Additionally, it rules puzzles, gossip, and mental activity. Mercury is the planet of thought and ideas.

Communication often requires an individual to move to different locations, so Gemini is associated with travel undertaken with a practical purpose in mind. It is the sign of busyness, taking care of the routine matters that are the necessities of life.

Bringing Up a Young Gemini

A parent should use fanciful and imaginative ways to get on a Gemini child's wavelength. Any kind of personal contact through words, ideas, gossip, or philosophy is a lifeline to a Gemini and turns a little tyke into a happy, inspiring, and devoted person. Geminis love it when they are given a lot of attention, and they enjoy learning about almost any subject.

Young Geminis should be taught how to distinguish between illusion and reality since they tend to live in a world where imagination and actuality are so mixed together that it is hard for them to determine where one ends and the other begins. These children will enjoy learning to communicate, read, and speak several languages. In fact, they can easily become multilingual if spoken to in different languages from an early age.

Teaching a Gemini child to slow down a little can be difficult, but it will help her blossom into a more focused adult. Geminis tend to skim the surface and may avoid finishing a chore or an assignment simply because they have moved on to the next thing that has piqued their interest.

More than anything, Gemini children need to be understood. They are naturally honest and will avoid telling the truth only as a defense mechanism when they feel misunderstood.

The Gemini Child

The typical Gemini child:

* is happy, bright, and alert
* may have trouble falling asleep
* usually learns to read quickly
* is extremely talkative
* can be quite adventurous
* will become cranky if tired
* moves quickly
* may be a tattler
* loves singing and gabbing
* needs lots of toys and games
* is friendly to adults
* is good with his hands
* sometimes has an imaginary friend

Gemini As Parent

The typical Gemini parent:

- is able to tune in to a child's world
- encourages creative expression
- is not a strict disciplinarian
- has a sense of humor
- promotes educational goals
- sets high standards
- is considered "cool" by her children's friends

Health

Geminis need to be careful of problems such as asthma, bronchitis, and the flu. This is because they tend to be nervous types who keep going even when overtired. They can become very run down, and their resistance is affected if they don't get enough rest. But they hate to be confined to bed! They sometimes have a problem taking good care of themselves because they are constantly on the go and often forget to adhere to regular eating and sleeping schedules. They must therefore try to establish a healthy routine and balance, which will reduce their erratic energy levels. Gemini "rules" the arms, hands, and shoulders; care must be taken when lifting weights or rushing to accomplish a chore.

FAMOUS GEMINIS

Mary Cassatt

Joan Collins

Bob Dylan

Clint Eastwood

Ralph Waldo Emerson

Michael J. Fox

Judy Garland

Bob Hope

Angelina Jolie

John F. Kennedy

Nicole Kidman

Cyndi Lauper

Tara Lipinski

Marilyn Monroe

Mary-Kate and Ashley Olsen

Cole Porter

Joan Rivers

Maurice Sendak

Brooke Shields

Donald Trump

Queen Victoria

Walt Whitman

Gene Wilder

Venus Williams

Frank Lloyd Wright

"Astrology is a science in itself, and contains an illuminating body of knowledge. It has taught me many things, and I am greatly in debt to it."

—ALBERT EINSTEIN

CANCER
June 21–July 22

CANCER
June 21–July 22

Planet: Moon

Element: Water

Quality: Cardinal

Day: Monday

Season: summer

Colors: silver, mauve, smoke gray

Plants: moonflower, water lily, chamomile

Perfume: sandalwood

Gemstones: moonstone, pearl, opal, hematite

Metal: silver

Personal qualities: Caring, tenacious, sensitive, intuitive, and practical

KEYWORDS

We call the following words "keywords" because they can help you unlock the core meaning of the astrological sign of Cancer. Each keyword represents issues and ideas that are of supreme importance and prominence in the lives of people born with Cancer as their Sun sign. You will usually find that a Cancer embodies at least one of these keywords in the way she makes a living:

*nurturing • fertile • clairvoyant • protective • heredity • farming
emotions • moods • consumerism • feelings • intuitions
wax and wane • reflect • respond • adapt • habits • cycles
motherhood • unconditional love • our past • cooking*

home making • passivity • memories of childhood • caregiving
secrets • conservation • leadership • love of comfort • patriotism
antiques • surrogacy • women's issues

Cancer's Symbolic Meaning

The symbol for Cancer is the Crab. Cancerians have a tendency to feel insecure at times, and when they experience this emotion they want to withdraw into their own version of a crab's protective shell. A crab carries its home on its back wherever it goes, and in much the same way, a Cancerian strives to make a metaphorical home out of even the most temporary surroundings.

The desire to nurture and protect loved ones is very strong in every Cancer and is borne out by the sign's designation as the Great Mother. The issue of people providing or failing to provide material support will be a central focus of every person born during the time of the sign of Cancer.

Cancer is one of the four Cardinal signs of the zodiac (the other three are Aries, Libra, and Capricorn). Cardinal signs are the first signs in each season. Thus, those born under these signs are initiators and act according to their aims and goals. Although they can be gentle and shy, they are also tenacious, and will fight hard to get what they want. But because they are quiet and well mannered, they are able to accomplish their aims without seeming to be pushy or demanding.

Additionally, Cancer is one of the three Water signs (the other two being Scorpio and Pisces). People whose signs fall into this group are highly imaginative and emotional. Cancer is the Water sign concerned with protection, caring, and comfort. Cancerians are legendary for their ability to nurture people and projects, for they sense the needs of others on an emotional level. However, they need to remember that meeting their own emotional needs is just as important. Often, they must be able to nurture themselves, for they are so good at nurturing others that those other people forget that Cancerians, too, need similar attention.

Cancerians would do well to remember that while they may not be as strong as those around them think they are, they are certainly strong enough to do what has to be done to make their dreams come true. They must resist withdrawing into their shell if they start to feel insecure. Their usual courage, patience, and gentle energy are more than they need to make their life what they will.

Recognizing a Cancer

People who exhibit the physical characteristics distinctive of the sign of Cancer have expressive eyes, a round "moon-shaped" face, and soft skin. Every mood, emotion, and fleeting response shows in the changing features of the sensitive Cancerian face. Those born under this sign are usually top-heavy, and their arms and legs tend to be long in relation to the rest of their body. They can often be on the plump side, especially later in life.

Cancer's Typical Behavior and Personality Traits

* is desirous of material comforts
* is extremely clairvoyant
* wears clothes that feel protective
* is a bit shy (not a show-off)
* is private about personal life
* is wonderful with children
* is introspective and emotional
* possesses a shrewd business sense
* enjoys good food and wine
* is protective of friends and family
* is patient and cautious with decisions
* gets her feelings hurt easily
* is dreamy, subtle, and intuitive

What Makes a Cancer Tick?

More than those born under any other sign, Cancerians are driven by feelings and intuition. Even though they are intelligent, practical people, they use their feelings as a sort of radar, and a great many of their decisions are based on this radar. While highly sensitive in the way they behave toward others, Cancerians are usually most sensitive when it comes to their own feelings. They are easily hurt by actions or attitudes that other signs are likely to dismiss. Hurt a Cancer and there is a chance that he will sulk.

The Cancer Personality Expressed Positively

Cancerians who possess high self-esteem and confidence may not seem much different from those who do not. But they, themselves, will certainly know the difference. The ability to sympathize with a friend's problems and still feel comfortable with their own success is a sign that Cancerians are able to balance their emotions, expressing their true nature in a positive way.

On a Positive Note

Cancers displaying the positive characteristics associated with their sign also tend to be:

* savvy
* kind
* warm
* compassionate
* nurturing
* thoughtful
* caring and sensitive
* introspective
* intuitive

The Cancer Personality Expressed Negatively

Moodiness, sulkiness, and an unwillingness to be open with others about their problems are just a few ways in which Cancerians express their personality in a negative way. These characteristics may surface when they are feeling bad about themselves or unequal to what is expected of them. Cancerians who don't feel good about themselves may become secretive or even deceptive.

Negative Traits

Cancers displaying the negative characteristics associated with their sign also tend to be:

- possessive
- controlling
- crabby
- too easily hurt
- sensitive to criticism
- manipulative
- overpowering
- selfish
- defensive

Ask a Cancer If...

Ask a Cancer if she'll listen if you want to share intimate feelings or events of a confidential nature but don't wish to be judged. Cancers pride themselves on being both empathetic and trustworthy and will listen to your problems or concerns with an open mind and an open heart. They also have the gift of giving counsel without lecturing, and will offer that service if you ask. If not, they will simply listen or provide a shoulder to cry on.

Cancers As Friends

There is no one who is more giving than a Cancer who feels secure emotionally. However, when those born under the sign of the Crab feel insecure, they are totally unable to give, and their resulting behavior can confuse friends who have come to depend on them at critical times.

On the Cancer's part, his sensitivity can lead to emotional moments with friends and his feelings being hurt. Cancerians are reluctant to tell anyone about their own needs for fear that the people they care about will let them down.

Cancerians have long memories. While they would be able to forgive a friend who was unable to be there for them, they would never forget what happened. In general, Cancerians like people who will support their emotional needs when necessary—and when they find this, they'll reciprocate.

Looking for Love

Cancerians may be attracted to an individual who reminds them of someone they used to care about. They tend to be highly romantic and dramatic in their love life, and will respond to honest warmth and affection. They can easily become tenaciously attached to someone who has no intention of making a commitment and therefore cannot return their feelings. They believe in falling in love at first sight, and if they meet someone without experiencing this sensation, it may be hard for them to believe that the person is really meant for them. Cancerians think that magic is a big part of romance, so if this element is missing, there may be little chance of a relationship getting off the ground. Also, Cancerians sometimes hold back because they fear rejection and, therefore, may lose out on their quest for love.

Shyness can be Cancer's obstacle to finding love. Even when Cancerians think someone they like may feel the same way, it can be difficult for them to summon the courage to speak up. They are not the sort to casually meet someone and trust that the connection has the potential to go further. Nor are they the type for going out every night. They are real homebodies, and will rarely make the first move. Love may just have to come knock on their door or they may meet a romantic interest through family or close friends. Once Cancerians have found a love interest, they will put that person first. They enjoy looking after the one they love and will "mother" them in some way. It's difficult for Cancerians to understand that a lover could consider this sort of treatment smothering. To them, it is simply love.

Finding That Special Someone

In the search for a love interest, comfort is a key factor. Cancerians are rarely happy barhopping or participating in the online dating scene. Rather, they are more likely to find themselves drawn to someone they meet at work, church, or a party given by a friend. Sometimes they find that the person of their dreams has been under their nose all the time—a friend or an associate.

First Dates

An ideal first date for Cancer is likely to involve a home-cooked meal or other domestic trappings. While this type of date may seem too emotionally intimate for some, Cancerians know how to make the experience non-threatening. Other favorable venues include a stroll on the beach, a trip to an amusement park, or an evening spent in an intimate jazz or comedy club. Cancerians are more interested in the company than the accoutrements—another expression of their down-to-earth attitude and spirit.

Cancer in Love

When Cancerians are with a partner, they should feel at home and have no need to be anywhere else.

They should spend time making their home into the kind of nest where a great relationship can be nurtured and grow strong. When they do set out on the road with a lover, they should visit a place from their past, or go to a hotel that feels like a home away from home. Cancerians are sentimental and enjoy showering their lover with attention. They show affection freely, but may restrict kissing and cuddling to private time.

Undying Love

At the first sign of ridicule or criticism, Cancerians will retreat, deeply hurt. Any problems Cancerians have in their love life are probably the result of childhood experiences. Cancer and his partner might come from completely different upbringings or one or both may have had serious traumas as children. If a Cancer is unable to forgive—especially his mother—he should consider professional counseling. If a Cancer is unable to forgive, his romantic relationships will be perpetually sabotaged by unresolved emotional problems.

Expectations in Love

Issues of mothering and nurturing are important in any Cancer's life. They may be looking for someone to take care of them or may be repelled by anyone who needs to be taken care of in some way. It may be hard to find a partner who shares a Cancer's views on children and child rearing. They are traditionalists, and if their own upbringing was happy, they will use it as their model.

Cancerians need to know that they are with someone who loves them and upon whom they can depend. This is paramount; they need to be supported, nurtured, and loved unconditionally. Although they are strong and capable people, they sometimes feel extremely vulnerable, and need to nurture their partner in order to make themselves feel safe and strong. They should be on the lookout for someone who embodies the same loving, gentle qualities. If that kind of relationship is not attractive to a Cancer, she may equate intensity, uncertainty, and even danger with passion and love, due to a difficult, dysfunctional upbringing.

What Cancerians Look For

Cancerians need a partner who appreciates their hard work, their nurturing personality, and their involvement with family. Totally devoted once they commit to a love affair, they expect the same kind of loyalty in return. Cancerians need to be needed. Cancerians like to have others—whether they be children, best friends, or family members—around them. A couple may even work closely together, and when they do, the others involved in the business can become like family to them.

If Cancerians Only Knew...

If Cancerians only knew how strong and dependable they appear to others, they wouldn't worry about letting someone close to them, especially a love interest, get a peek at their vulnerabilities. For the most part, other people perceive only the powerful will and self-discipline of Cancer. Yet Cancerians often feel weak simply because they are so sensitive. This is odd, since it is precisely that sensitivity that gives them the ability to reach out to other people in ways that are so special and so spiritually pure.

Marriage

The past is very important to Cancerians. Their family history is especially so, either as a source of pride or because of a painful experience that continues to affect them as if it just happened. Either way, Cancerians want to relate what is going on in the present to something they have known in the past. By doing this, or by simply sticking with the familiar, they are able to feel secure.

The person who contemplates marrying a typical Cancer must realize that that person will want to be the dominant partner and will expect total devotion. That said, the person who pairs up with a Cancer can expect consideration, prosperity, and a strong sense of being part of a family. The contented Cancerian will never let a partner down, stressing a sense of belonging as well as love.

Cancer's Opposite Sign

Capricorn, the Goat, is the opposite sign of Cancer. It is a hard and flinty sign possessing many of the strengths that Cancer isn't likely to have. But it is through those very differences that Capricorn can teach Cancer to be strong and emotionally self-sufficient. Capricorn, in turn, can learn from Cancer the ways to be sensitive and caring, as well as how to accept the emotional nurturing that Capricorn is likely to require.

Pairing Up

In general, if people display the characteristics typical of their sign, intimate relationships between a Cancer and another individual can be described as follows:

Cancer with Cancer:	Harmonious, if there isn't too much emotional baggage
Cancer with Leo:	Harmonious, so long as Leo gets plenty of attention
Cancer with Virgo:	Harmonious, with both partners supporting each other's dreams
Cancer with Libra:	Difficult, but enhanced by shared life view and goals
Cancer with Scorpio:	Harmonious—deeply sensual and eternally romantic
Cancer with Sagittarius:	Turbulent but joyous, with lots of fights and makeup sessions
Cancer with Capricorn:	Difficult, although there is much for each to learn from the other
Cancer with Aquarius:	Turbulent, especially if there are political and philosophical differences
Cancer with Pisces:	Harmonious, with shared sensitivity and romantic idealism
Cancer with Aries:	Difficult but exciting, though Aries needs to be tender

| Cancer with Taurus: | Harmonious in the extreme—a match made in paradise |
| Cancer with Gemini: | Harmonious, if Gemini gives Cancer plenty of emotional space |

If Things Don't Work Out

In modern psychology emphasis has been placed on getting in touch with childhood experiences. Only recently has equal emphasis been placed on taking responsibility for who you are now. Cancer needs to learn from the past but live in the present.

Cancerians' relationships reflect their emotional intelligence. How Cancer and his partner express their emotions will determine how well things are going. If a relationship breaks up, Cancer will shoulder most of the blame.

Cancer at Work

Cancerians need to feel that they are doing more than just a job; they want to feel more like they have found a home. They like work that reminds them of the work done by their family in the past. A sense of continuity is very important to them. Family and those who care deeply about them can help their job and career in some way. Cancerians may also work out of their home.

Cancers must feel emotionally comfortable and secure in the workplace. This means having lots of family photos and some special mementos displayed, lots of snacks and water handy, and bins and boxes to organize clutter.

A woman, matters related to women and children, mothering, mother figures, and possibly the Cancer's own mother can affect her career in an important way. If relations with women and a Cancer's mother are good, the career will benefit. If not, there can be emotional troubles that appear at work, so a Cancer should be aware of and try to heal the issues in that relationship.

Cancerians must also be on good terms with coworkers to feel secure and get their career moving properly. People who are considered "family" at work and how Cancerians have been getting along with them are very important to their professional life. If those relationships have been difficult, a Cancer must take action to make things better. Until things have been straightened out, the Cancer's career will feel blocked.

Typical Occupations

Occupations that Cancerians are well suited for address the basic needs of families, from spirituality to housework. They make excellent chefs and caterers and also housekeepers. Many find their calling in real estate.

All jobs with children or that involve nurturing people would be beneficial to them. Thus, they may succeed in anything from social work to nursing. And working with animals and gardens will be favored by them. Cancerians' nurturing capabilities also apply to fostering new business projects that are struggling to survive. Excellent organizers with a sense of value and economics, they are often successful in industry.

Those born under the sign of the Crab have an intuitive sense that makes them good counselors and journalists. The sign's love of the past makes some Cancerians great history buffs, and others astute collectors of antiques and curios. True to their native element, some of the people born under this Water sign become involved in marine activities.

Behavior and Abilities at Work

In the workplace, a typical Cancer:

- is loyal and efficient
- excels as either a leader or a team member

* gets along well with others in the workplace
  * may be resistant to new ideas
  * has the company's interests at heart

Cancer As Employer

A typical Cancer boss:

  * drives a hard bargain but is fair
  * treats employees like family
  * expects employees to dress nicely
  * takes work seriously
  * does not like silliness
  * focuses on making money
  * possesses an excellent memory
  * likes to reward loyalty

Cancer As Employee

A typical Cancer employee:

  * likes to be given responsibility
  * has goals of increasing income
  * expects to be rewarded for hard work
  * is good at sales and marketing
  * will have a calm and considerate personality
  * uses intuition more than logic
  * enjoys being part of a "family"

Cancer As Coworker

Making others feel like they are part of the group is crucial for Cancerians. However, Cancerians may sometimes pull back from having close ties in the workplace. They may fear sharing the intimate details of their own personal life with others. Since they feel vulnerable to criticism or judgment, Cancerians are less likely than other signs to gossip.

Details, Details

Cancers thrive on details as long as these small, daily elements of work, and life for that matter, support a bigger, more comprehensive plan of action. They are not overly logical, and yet they have an instinct for statistics, dates, and budgetary items. Thanks to their natural talent for organization, Cancers rarely get bogged down in details. They are much more likely to see them as the underpinnings of an important and profitable enterprise.

In the workplace, Cancers do not feel as though they are "above" handling the small details that make up a big project. Dogged and determined, they will slog away at the difficult elements of a project, never worrying about whether or not they will end up getting credit for the final results. This has nothing to do with a lack of ego on their part. They know that they have the ability to work as a team member better than many of their coworkers.

Money

Whether a Cancer lives in a cave or a castle, making it beautiful, comfortable, and safe would be money well spent. Collecting original art would feed a Cancer's soul, something that is necessary to achieve true wealth and success.

Cancer's financial resources are likely to come from or be connected to organizations related to the home, products for the home, the past, or family values. If a Cancer wants to enter any lotteries, he would do better to enter with close friends and family. Numbers important to family members would be the most likely to be lucky. A Cancer should try to profit from the advice of family and people from the past and from long-term investments. Real estate, especially a property a Cancer or his family intends to live on, is a good bet. Any improvements that a Cancer makes to where he lives will be good investments, too.

At Home

In order to nurture the ones they love, Cancerians must first feel secure. They want their home to be comfortable, a true sanctuary where they can relax and enjoy family life and activities. Because Cancer is the Cardinal Water sign, it follows that emotion in action is the key to understanding how Cancerians relax.

Behavior and Abilities at Home

Cancer typically:

* enjoys feeling safe and relaxed
* is handy with home improvements
* enjoys entertaining guests
* has lots of cookbooks
* has plants or a garden
* may have collections of family heirlooms
* doesn't like to throw things away

Leisure Interests

Cancerians may join health clubs, but they prefer yoga, swimming, and meditation to weight lifting and aerobics. They enjoy relaxing on the beach with a good book. And they love to just hang out with friends and family, enjoying a good meal, surrounded by the warmth of a contented atmosphere.

The typical Cancer enjoys the following pastimes:

* gardening or tending plants
* playing with his pets
* collecting antiques
* engaging in team sports or playing games
* keeping a journal
* boating, sailing, or swimming

Cancerian Likes

* anyone who has a kind heart
* mementos from family and friends
* comfort food
* shopping sprees
* history and psychology books
* sentimental gifts
* birthday cards
* old friends
* a beautiful home
* cuddly pajamas or soft blankets

Cancerian Dislikes

* harsh words
* fast food
* people who forget important dates
* not being acknowledged for her contribution
* talking to strangers
* a messy home
* having to respond quickly, without time to think
* moving
* not having money
* being nagged at or lectured

The Secret Side of Cancer

Cancerians are often affected by the time of day they decide to do something. Plans made at night become harder to make real in the daytime and vice versa. If they find themselves forgetting to put the plans of last night into practice the next day, they must be as patient and forgiving of themselves as they would be with the mistakes made by a child.

The Moon

The Moon, which is considered a planet in astrology, is associated with the sign of Cancer. The way in which the Moon seems to change size and shape, along with the Moon's effect on the constantly shifting ocean tides, resembles Cancer's ever-changing moods; however, the Moon's changes are a lot more predictable.

Astrologers of old associated the Moon with our emotions, our emotional intelligence, our intuition, and the expression of all of these things. Because it changes shape from full to new on a schedule so close to that of a woman's menstrual cycle, the Moon is associated with women, fertility, planting, childbirth, mothering, and nurturing in general. It also rules the relationship between mother and child. Watching over us all the time, though not always seen, the Moon represents our unconscious attitudes, patterns, and past conditioning. This celestial body rules the breast and stomach.

Bringing Up a Young Cancer

Cancerian children love to use their imaginations and are easy to get along with, provided they are given lots of warmth, approval, and attention. Usually gentle, complacent souls, they most of all are sure of what they want and need.

Cancerian youths need to feel free to express their emotions through art, music, writing, or any other form of creativity. They need plenty of outlets for their vivid imaginations. Thus, young Cancerians should be taught the basic techniques of any art form and given the proper materials and space within which to be creative.

The parents of a Cancerian child must find a way not to be too possessive or overprotective. They may worry too much about their little Cancerian child, as children born under this sign are deeply sensitive to emotional hurts and rejections and are prone to withdrawing into their little shells.

If the child feels unloved or neglected, she could grow up to be a reclusive, withdrawn adult who is overly self-protective and reluctant to trust or get too close to other people.

Like those born during the other Water signs, Pisces and Scorpio, Cancer children can be very intuitive; many may display what appears to be psychic abilities. Their caregivers need to value this while guiding them to develop their logical faculties too.

The Cancer Child

The typical Cancer child:

- likes to be hugged
- may cry a lot
- changes moods from day to day
- likes to save money
- can manipulate to get what he wants
- loves mealtime
- is fascinated by picture books
- gets her feelings hurt easily
- withdraws if unhappy
- can play alone for hours
- conjures up imaginary playmates
- likes traditional fairy tales and myths

Cancer As a Parent

The typical Cancer parent:

- likes to organize birthday parties
- supports creativity
- is overprotective
- is very reassuring when fears arise

* enjoys playing with the kids
* will do anything to help
* displays affection

Health

Cancerians are emotional types who may suffer from stomach problems when under stress. They tend to bottle things up and are prone to ulcers. As they do not like to burden other people with their problems, they tend to suffer in silence. Typical Cancerians need material security, plenty of affection, and a sense that they are needed. As long as these needs are met, they can handle a lot.

Wholesome food and regular meals are important to Cancer. Overindulgence in sweets can result in extra weight gained in later years. Since theirs is a water sign, Cancerians should try taking long, warm baths to relax.

FAMOUS CANCERS

Louis Armstrong

Bill Blass

Mel Brooks

Bill Cosby

Tom Cruise

Diana, Princess of Wales

Harrison Ford

Bob Fosse

John Glenn

Tom Hanks

Ernest Hemingway

Frida Kahlo

Lindsay Lohan

Nelson Mandela

George Orwell

Gilda Radner

Ginger Rogers

Carlos Santana

Carly Simon

Sylvester Stallone

Ringo Starr

Meryl Streep

Robin Williams

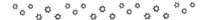

"We are born at a given moment, in a given place and, like vintage years of wine, we have the qualities of the year and of the season of which we are born."

—CARL GUSTAV JUNG

LEO
July 23–August 22

LEO

July 23–August 22

Planet: Sun

Element: Fire

Quality: Fixed

Day: Sunday

Season: summer

Colors: gold, orange, yellow

Plants: marigold, sunflower, nasturtium

Perfume: orange blossom

Gemstones: amber, carnelian, citrine, ruby

Metal: gold

Personal qualities: Creative, dramatic, proud, organized, and romantic

Keywords

We call the following words "keywords" because they can help you unlock
the core meaning of the astrological sign of Leo. Each keyword represents
issues and ideas that are of supreme importance and prominence in the lives
of people born with Leo as their Sun sign. You will usually find that every
Leo embodies at least one of these keywords in the way he makes a living:

self-assertion • creativity • a place in the Sun • recognition
theatricality • hobbies • leadership • romance • pleasures
fun • hospitality • openheartedness • appreciation • beach resorts
fame • playfulness • entertainment • children • luck • gambling

sports • acting out • games • performance • sun worshipping
love affair • regal bearing • self-love • hero or heroine
prizewinner • golden objects • show business

Leo's Symbolic Meaning

Leo is the sign of the creative organizers of the zodiac. Practically no one is as good as they are at recognizing the solution to a problem and organizing the means to solve it. It is this ability that gives rise to Leo's reputation as a great leader. Like all leaders, most Leos feel more comfortable when they are telling others what has to be done rather than taking care of the routine details themselves. They get annoyed with themselves for this trait, but not for long, because Leos like themselves a lot. They put themselves where there is much that needs to be done and they associate themselves with the right group of people so that their creative input is always welcome, even if they do not always jump in and get their hands dirty.

The symbol for Leo is the strong and proud male lion, a most appropriate symbol. Not only is a group of lions referred to as a "pride," but also the importance of personal pride to those born during the time of Leo cannot be overstated. They do not want to be connected to anyone or anything that they do not feel is up to their high personal standards.

Showing us all how things are done is a special gift that Leos possess. This is why they have such a knack for drama—acting, the arts and music, or any form of display. Their generosity requires them to create situations and objects that will benefit and entertain them and those they consider worthy to be connected with them.

Leo is one of the four Fixed Sun signs of astrology (the other three are Taurus, Scorpio, and Aquarius). Fixed signs are stable, resolute, and determined. They represent the force of holding steady. Being a Fixed sign makes Leos loyal, stubborn, and proud.

Leo is also a Fire sign, one of three (Aries and Sagittarius are the other two). Fire signs are primarily energetic, enthusiastic, and impulsive.

Leos are legendary for their ability to help and protect those who acknowledge them as special people. They gain a sense of their own self-worth by giving what they think others need from them. However, it is important that they remember that they, too, need help and protection. Leos are usually too prideful to ask for help.

Recognizing a Leo

People who exhibit the physical characteristics distinctive of the sign Leo look noble. They may seem tall and possess a majestic countenance. A Leo knows how to dress to impress. Leo's inner sense of royalty exudes dignity, elegance, and class. A Leo's hair can appear to be like a lion's mane—a feature of pride that catches the attention of others. Leos move with a natural athletic grace.

Leo's Typical Behavior and Personality Traits

* needs to be admired
* is trusting and loyal
* uses charm to get what she wants
* likes to show off
* is trusting
* likes excitement
* is generous
* has elegant tastes
* is popular
* gives and expects respect
* is generous with affection
* is a leader

What Makes a Leo Tick?

Leos may worry that they are not as proud, powerful, or good a leader as they wish they were, and that people who matter to them will discover this fact. At times they need to fall back on the "fake it till you make it" philosophy. Sometimes, even the best of leaders must put on an act to get the job done. Leos find it very difficult to be a team player, since they feel it is their lot to lead others.

The Leo Personality Expressed Positively

At their very best, Leos are an intelligent, creative force wherever they operate. Their ability to solve problems with a combination of optimism and common sense is a marvel to behold. Leos have a rare talent for being both commanding and friendly at the same time. When Leo is happy, he makes the whole world around him a bit sunnier.

On a Positive Note

Leos displaying the positive characteristics associated with their sign also tend to be:

* attractive and demonstrative
* positive thinking
* dignified and charming
* honest and loyal
* proud of their homes
* warm, friendly, and generous with gifts
* courageous and bold
* responsible and mature
* adoring of loved ones

The Leo Personality Expressed Negatively

When Leos are working on projects for others to look at, their audience's feedback becomes very important to them. If their creations are not acknowledged or praised to the hilt, their pride will be hurt. As a result, they might forget their usual kindhearted ways and may even try to use their power or influence to sway the opinions of others. They may sulk if attention is not paid to them or to their efforts.

Negative Traits

Leos displaying the negative characteristics associated with their sign also tend to be:

* superior in attitude
* status conscious
* smug and conceited
* arrogant and self-involved
* stubborn or willful
* overdramatic
* brooding and vengeful
* judgmental about appearances
* overeager to impress

Ask a Leo If...

Ask a Leo if you need help organizing a project or enterprise of any sort. The task can be big or small, complicated or relatively easy, but no matter what it is, Leo has a plan for how to get it done better, faster, more economically, and even with more style. She believes that her way is the only way, and will probably tell you so. Leo may criticize your way of handling things, but always in a pleasing manner!

Leos As Friends

Leos as friends are caring, thoughtful, warm, and fun to be with. They love their friends and need to feel proud of them. They are generous with resources and hospitality, expecting friends to show their gratitude in kind. Leos dislike cheapness in any form and are unlikely to make friends with people whom they perceive as being cheap. In general, Leos like their friends to be successful, but not so successful as to take any attention away from Leo's limelight! A friend who has strong personal aspirations or ambitions that compete with Leo's may find it impossible to have a close and trusting relationship.

A friend who fails a Leo by criticizing something she has done or belittling something she cares deeply about may be dropped like a hot potato.

Looking for Love

Leos need to put themselves into the most positive situations to find love. If they are in a place where they are happy, they will create an incredible relationship. If they are in a place where their energy has to be used just to keep things going, they could lose one of their most valuable possessions: their time. If a Leo does not have a good relationship, the reason most likely has to do with ego. The Leo may be too concerned with status to be able to be with people who are good for her. To Leo, love is a dramatic ideal, and sometimes this factor overshadows the possibility of romance with someone who may not look, act, or seem like someone Leo believes she should be with. Leos are not shallow people, but they do set the bar very high. Male Leos seem to have no trouble attracting women, while female Leos attract many men with their natural beauty and liveliness.

Leos don't endorse the "friends first, lovers later" philosophy. They are often likely to fall in love at first sight, or at least on the first date! For them, romance is more likely to flower from a chance meeting, by coincidence, or through paths crossed by accident. It is common for Leos to transfer all their ideas and ideals about romance to a new love affair, believing that the one they have fallen in love with possesses all the traits and characteristics they desire, even if this isn't the case. In fact, the biggest disappointment Leos in love can suffer is to discover that the one they love isn't the paragon of romantic virtues they first envisioned.

Finding That Special Someone

Leos have to take the lead to create and improve the kind of relationship they want; they should not expect to simply sit back and let things happen. It would be good for a Leo to keep things organized and moving in terms of making dates and plans.

First Dates

The perfect first date for Leo can be attending a sporting event or going to a movie. Leos don't need the quiet intimacy of a dimly lit restaurant to create a spirit of emotional intimacy and romance. They love to be in the midst of a crowd. They are often movie buffs as well, so an evening spent watching a new comedy over popcorn could also be their style.

Leos are active people, and they enjoy being out in the sunshine, so a good first date could be sailing, surfing, or just lying in the sun. A stroll on the beach at sunset sets a romantic mood.

Leo in Love

Leos are the true romantics of the zodiac. They can enjoy all kinds of fun things and creative expressions together with their partners. It is rewarding for a Leo to actively pursue creative projects with a love interest. Attending creative classes together, visiting museums, and going to art galleries, movies, dance recitals, concerts, and the theater are all pursuits that light a Leo's fire. A long vacation is also a perfect way to stimulate Leo's romantic nature.

Undying Love

For Leo, problems in a relationship may be the result of not making time for fun and romance. Children may be the problem, or views on children may conflict, especially regarding the conditions that have to be present before children can be brought into the world and reared properly. Trouble in a Leo's relationships could also be caused by problems related to organization, responsibility, and leadership. If Leo finds that there are many essential tasks that neither partner is good at, then both must try their best to do them together.

Expectations in Love

Leo wants a partner who enhances her own image and who enjoys being in the spotlight as much as she does. Leo's partner must be good-looking and have great taste, but should not detract attention from Leo. Leo wants a partner who will place her on a pedestal and believe in her dreams with all of his heart. Leo loves good manners, expects to be treated like royalty, and needs total commitment of faithfulness and adoration from a loved one. Affection is an important factor in any Leo relationship. Leos need to be shown in all ways that they are loved.

Leo's partner must enjoy all aspects of entertaining and must have the creative flair for making their home a beautiful showcase. With the right partner, a Leo will rise in social status due to her generous hospitality, enthusiasm, and persistence for excellence. Consequently, Leo's fire will make her partner shine, too. Despite having a large ego, Leo is dedicated to being the ideal partner, too.

What Leos Look For

Because appearance and style mean a lot to Leo, these may often be the first things he searches for in a romantic partner. But there are many other traits that are important to him, so he is not likely to judge on looks alone. Leos require someone whose enthusiasm and zest for life matches their own. They are not interested in people who are emotional downers or too needy, no matter how attractive they might otherwise be. Healthy self-esteem is a trait Leos admire in others.

If Leo Only Knew...

If Leo only knew that even the greatest ruler has to listen to the advice of others. An unrestrained ego can do more damage to Leo and her creations than any enemy. Leos need to realize that they cannot always be the star of the show and that there are times when it is better for them to follow the example of others rather than always having to lead the way. They should know that it is not only their masterful personality but also their sunniness, kind disposition, and fair-minded approach to life that attracts the admiration and love of the people around them.

Marriage

Leos and their partners should create projects together that have a life of their own, such as business enterprises, or works of art, such as tapestries, plays, sculpture, novels, clothing, movies, music, and other similar things. One of the most creative things people can produce is a child, and Leos love children. Just being connected with children and things related to them brings Leos much joy. Add to that the previously mentioned businesses and artistic enterprises, and even material benefits can result.

No matter how busy a Leo is, she must make time for romantic interludes. A relationship where there is no romance is in danger of ending.

Leo's Opposite Sign

Aquarius, the Water Carrier, is the complementary opposite sign of Leo. There may be tough relations between them, but Aquarius can show Leo how to share without needing appreciation, and how to give the center stage to others. This can be a big challenge for Leo, but it is a way in which he can learn to stand alone and value himself. Aquarius does not approach life from Leo's sunny perspective, and in this way, the Lion can be a good example for Aquarius to copy.

Pairing Up

In general, if people display the characteristics typical of their sign, intimate relationships between a Leo and another individual can be described as follows:

Leo with Leo:	Harmonious, so long as both are willing to share the spotlight
Leo with Virgo:	Harmonious, but personality differences need a wide berth
Leo with Libra:	Harmonious; the equivalent of a lifelong party
Leo with Scorpio:	Difficult, since both are equally stubborn
Leo with Sagittarius:	Harmonious, as friends as well as lovers
Leo with Capricorn:	Turbulent, if Capricorn won't relinquish the purse strings
Leo with Aquarius:	Difficult, but the partners are able to illuminate life lessons for each other
Leo with Pisces:	Turbulent, if Pisces can't stand up to Leo's demands
Leo with Aries:	Harmonious; a lifelong romance and undying passion
Leo with Taurus:	Difficult, but with deeply sensual overtones
Leo with Gemini:	Harmonious; a partnership of ideas as well as romance
Leo with Cancer:	Harmonious, if differences bring out the best in each other

If Things Don't Work Out

The partner who is unfaithful to Leo, or who walks out on a serious love affair, will leave behind a very wounded person. It will take Leo months to recover from such a deep hurt and may make him very wary of risking serious love again. Leo will need to heal not only a broken heart, but a broken spirit as well. A love affair that ends badly can greatly impact Leo's ego and self-esteem.

Leo at Work

It is good for a Leo to be creative, no matter what her job or career. This always requires her to look at what projects and tasks she tackles in a new way. A Leo should not just accept that she knows the best way to accomplish a goal at work. It is very important that a Leo does work that allows her to somehow express her ability to create solutions to problems and general improvements. Leo could even try to bring in someone, maybe even a young person, and explain the problem to him. The fresh look of his eyes may provide a surprising solution.

Although Leo has the ability to work as an effective team member, she doesn't necessarily have the temperament for it. She is accustomed to being the "idea person" on projects, as well as the dynamic force that gets the project done. Also, it is difficult for Leo to abdicate the role as authority figure, harder still to admit learning a better way of doing things from someone else. Other than creative input, Leo's best attribute in the workplace is a genius for organization.

Typical Occupations

A job in traditionally creative fields such as music, dance, acting, writing, design, or fashion would be wonderful for a Leo. Leos possess a strong creative and dramatic personality, and you will find many in the theater, television, and film industry. They become stars of stage or screen, talented musicians, or well-known painters, so a career opportunity in the arts could be pursued. Other jobs that may be good for Leo are investing, sports-related work, gaming of all kinds, and opportunities to display goods, either for ads or in the place where they are sold. Leos may also find that they are called on to do some public speaking, another opportunity to display their innate creativity.

Leos do well in careers where they can rise to the top. In the political arena, they keep going until they reach a powerful position. In business, you can find Leo as chairperson or president or on the board of directors. Leos are ambitious by nature, and prefer to take charge and delegate. Many Leos go into business for themselves.

Behavior and Abilities at Work

In the workplace, the typical Leo:

* must be in charge
* makes a good impression
* has many talents
* gives wonderful speeches
* can't admit mistakes
* likes to dress the part

Leo As Employer

A typical Leo boss:

* can create enthusiasm for a project
* cannot tolerate tardiness or failure
* is charming and gives compliments
* cannot have his authority undermined
* is generous with time and money
* takes the credit for successes

* instills confidence and devotion
* has a huge ego
* knows how to get the job done

Leo As Employee

A typical Leo employee:

* responds to genuine praise
* is very loyal and trustworthy
* needs to have his work recognized
* likes to prove that he is the best
* works hard to be promoted
* can create a congenial atmosphere
* likes to show off success

Leo As Coworker

Leos needs to be involved with people and in projects where they are able to use their leadership qualities. Whatever their job, they make sure they steal the limelight, which sometimes causes rifts with coworkers, even though they naturally get along well with others. Leos love to display pictures of places they have traveled, or of them at a memorable event. They need to inspire admiration, so they often display status symbols as well.

Details, Details

Because Leos' chief ability is leadership, it may be believed that they can't handle the details of a project, but this isn't the case. It is precisely because they are so good at balancing the importance of details with an ability to see the whole picture that they are successful. However, even though they make use of details in an admirable way, they can show disdain for them if they get in the way of a larger concept.

Leos can also be quite creative in work that requires physical labor. They don't believe in cutting corners and always adhere to the prescribed guidelines or safety standards. Leo often shows her inner strength when under the pressures of a deadline or crisis. Even in the most chaotic, stressful, and messy situations, Leo's ability to keep track of detailed information and use it to the best possible advantage shows just how helpful her organizational skills can be.

Time management is a Leo specialty. Leos are especially prolific leading a team effort that is deadline sensitive. Because of their natural leadership ability and gift for prioritizing tasks, Leos prove that to be detail oriented does not mean being shortsighted!

Money

Leos can benefit from taking calculated risks in the stock market and other legal forms of gambling, or from taking a chance on a new idea that comes as a creative inspiration. A Leo's good fortune can best come through having fun, enjoying love and romance, and being creative. If a Leo can look at even his routine tasks as pleasurable, it will bring into his life wealth and success in the fastest time possible.

Games, including sports, performing, creativity, and children, can benefit a Leo financially. A Leo is also in very good position to profit, not only from all these things, but also from taking a chance on a calculated risk or gamble. Investing, a more socially respectable form of gambling, is also favored. Leos enjoy spending lavishly and would be wise to keep to a strict budget most of the time.

At Home

Leo sees his home as his castle. Lavishing attention on its care, beautifying it, as well as showing it off to others are his ways of showing what it means to him.

Every Leo has at least one object at home that others might consider ostentatious. A Leo needs to be able to be comfortable and completely herself at home and will get anxious to the degree that this is not possible.

Behavior and Abilities at Home

Leo typically:

- is able to complete household odd jobs
- is king of his castle
- shows strength of character in emergencies
- offers comfort and affection to family
- has a taste for elegance in the home
- needs others to respect his space

Leisure Interests

Leos derive much benefit from allowing their creativity free rein. The rewards given to true artists are secondary in importance to the pleasure they get just from taking the time to make their art. Leos need to exercise their creative talents, in whatever manner they enjoy.

The typical Leo enjoys the following pastimes:

- watching competitive sports on TV
- reading celebrity biographies
- shopping for clothes
- keeping a journal
- going to concerts
- giving parties at home

Leo Likes

- a lot of action
- adoration and recognition

- being creative
- receiving gifts of gold
- famous people
- the theater
- an appreciative audience
- children and pets
- exotic food and restaurants
- warm places
- designer clothes

Leo Dislikes

- not being appreciated
- cold weather
- physical inactivity
- being ignored or not being chosen
- working behind the scenes
- cheap perfume
- being taken for granted
- being told she can't do something
- tacky furnishings
- eating every meal at home
- subtlety or subterfuge

The Secret Side of Leo

Privately, the typical Leo craves love more than anyone would ever guess. A true Leo is a person who wants to be on top, to be the one in charge, and to be listened to, without question. Yet, both the aspiration as well as the reality put great stress on Leo. While typical Leos may appear to be confident, especially when they take center stage, they have secret doubts about their true worth and may seriously undervalue themselves.

The Sun

The sign Leo is ruled by the planet the Sun. Though Sumerian and Babylonian astrologers knew that the Sun was a star, they counted it as a planet, the most important one. The ancient astrological symbol for the Sun, a dot in the center of a circle, shows they knew that the Sun was orbited by the planets. It also symbolizes us in the center of our personal "solar system" of friends, family, coworkers, and neighbors. The Sun gives light and life to our world, and in astrology the Sun symbolizes the ego. The planets revolve around the Sun, which is why it also rules celebrity, status, and the power to reign. The Sun's heat and light give life, and so the Sun represents fatherhood in a warm, giving, illuminating sense. It represents a father who gives life to his offspring, believes in the abilities of his creations, and is proud of them. The Sun rules our hearts.

Bringing Up a Young Leo

Most little Leos have turbulent emotions and often act out in dramatic ways. They always enjoy the limelight at school and often take the lead in tasks and activities.

The friendly Leo nature endears Leo children to everyone, including strangers. Since they are generally outgoing, they need to be taught discernment when it comes to talking to strangers.

Parents may find a bossy little Leo on their hands if they don't use enough discipline and convincing to impress the importance of homework and doing jobs around the house. It is good to reward a Leo, as she needs plenty of love, hugs, and praise for her achievements.

She should also be taught to handle her allowance, as she is likely to spend it frivolously at times. As it is in almost all things with a young Leo, what is taught is not as important as what caregivers and other teachers demonstrate in their interactions with adults. Leo children have an innate knowledge that what people say and what they do are often two different things. Young Leos can become surprisingly comfortable with and adept at stretching the truth to suit their purposes if the adults around them fail to demonstrate that duplicitous behavior whose purpose is the avoiding of hurt feelings is the only proper use of not telling the truth.

Leo children are naturally happiest when doing something physical. As they grow up, they will be attracted to the opposite sex, get huge crushes, and fall in and out of love. A parent of any Leo needs to understand that Leos can be overdramatic, especially about romance, so they should encourage them to tell the truth.

The Leo Child

The typical Leo child:

- does not like to sit still
- tries to be the center of attention
- loves games and playacting
- has a lot of energy
- is sunny and friendly
- is adventuresome and brave
- enjoys being catered to
- is generous with playmates
- dislikes being ignored
- loves parties and group endeavors
- is interested in romance from an early age
- will try to direct the actions of other children
- can sometimes stretch the truth a bit
- likes to pretend to be a parent or an authority

Leo As a Parent

The typical Leo parent:

- is encouraging and approachable
- allows children to make messes
- likes organizing children's activities
- encourages children to play sports
- is liberal with discipline
- expresses affection easily and often

Health

Typical Leos are happy, healthy, energetic people as long as they are loved. If for some reason they are not getting the attention or affection that they crave, Leos will complain. They can sometimes overindulge in rich food and wine, but too much of this is bad. Care should be taken when it comes to putting on weight. Leos should take care of their hearts and backs, as these are the parts of the body that Leo rules.

Whatever physical weaknesses he has, a typical Leo will enjoy only a brief period of rest before he is up again and on the go. To be out of commission for long is intolerable to a Leo.

FAMOUS LEOS

Ben Affleck

Tori Amos

Lucille Ball

Napoleon Bonaparte

Fidel Castro

Bill Clinton

Robert De Niro

Amelia Earhart

Henry Ford

Melanie Griffith

Alfred Hitchcock

Dustin Hoffman

Iman

Mick Jagger

Carl Jung

Jennifer Lopez

Madonna

Jacqueline Kennedy Onassis

Maxwell Parrish

Robert Redford

J.K. Rowling

Arnold Schwarzenegger

James Taylor

Charlize Theron

Andy Warhol

"The signs of the zodiac are karmic patterns; the planets are the looms, the will is the weaver."

—AUTHOR UNKNOWN

VIRGO
August 23–September 22

VIRGO
August 23–September 22

Planet: Mercury

Element: Earth

Quality: Mutable

Day: Wednesday

Season: summer

Colors: navy blue, gray, green, tan

Plants: fern, chrysanthemum, sage

Perfume: patchouli

Gemstones: apatite, aventurine, white opal, peridot

Metal: mercury

Personal qualities: Conservative, discreet, practical, intelligent, and detail oriented

Keywords

We call the following words "keywords" because they can help you unlock the core meaning of the astrological sign of Virgo. Each keyword represents issues and ideas that are of supreme importance and prominence in the lives of people born with Virgo as their Sun sign. You will usually find that every Virgo embodies at least one of these keywords in the way she makes a living:

thought • observation • study • analysis • discrimination
division into component parts • criticism • reason • logic
connection • adaptation • moving things about

---

spreading • making by hand • crafting • forming • detail
prediction • calculation • symbolism • translation
communication • speech • writing and reading

Virgo's Symbolic Meaning

Virgo is usually depicted as a young woman holding shafts of wheat. While Virgo is commonly thought of as "the virgin," it is important to note that in ancient times the word "virgin" actually had two meanings: it was used not only to refer to a sexually inexperienced individual, but also to describe an independent woman who did things on her own terms and over whom no man held dominion. Indeed, Virgos thrive when they are able to do things in their own way.

The dual meaning of the word "virgin" reflects the dual nature that most Virgos exhibit. Sometimes they are completely confident in their opinions and competence, but at other times they are as filled with self-doubt and naïveté as a young beginner. This aspect of their character correlates perfectly with the fact that Virgo is one of the four Mutable, or changeable, signs of astrology (the other three being Gemini, Pisces, and Sagittarius).

The Sun passes through the Mutable signs of the zodiac when we here on Earth are preparing for the change of seasons, and people born during the time of these Mutable signs are therefore considered to be highly adaptable under a variety of circumstances. Flexible and open to change, such individuals deal with each situation depending on the needs and desires of the moment. Virgos are more comfortable adapting to outside influences than they are imposing their will on others.

The shafts of wheat held by the strong young woman represent Virgo's connection with the Earth; this is key because Virgo is an Earth sign—one of three Sun signs focused on physical well-being and the practical matters of daily life (the other two Earth signs are Taurus and Capricorn). The element of Earth symbolizes logic, dependability, and a sense of duty to those

♍

who are considered valuable and worthy. People born during the time that the Sun is traveling through one of the three Earth signs are the most reliable and responsible. They have their feet on the ground and possess a practical gift for understanding the material world.

The wheat that Virgo holds is also symbolic of the harvest—the time of year during which a Virgo's birthday falls. In agrarian societies, harvesttime was the busiest and most important time of the year—hence, Virgo's hardworking tendencies.

Recognizing a Virgo

People who exhibit the physical characteristics distinctive of the sign of Virgo look neat and fastidious and have a pleasant, often quietly beautiful face. They are not usually noisy people or the kind to call attention to themselves on purpose, though their version of what looks right and proper is often unique, so that it appears as though they're dressing to confront other people's values—but they're not!

Virgo's Typical Behavior and Personality Traits

* is capable of analyzing situations in detail
* is basically shy, no matter how talkative
* is unsentimental and unemotional
* serves others in some way
* defines herself through work
* feels a little insecure
* notices and remembers details
* is efficient and orderly
* is helpful with practical matters
* does not express feelings easily
* can be critical or perfectionistic
* takes responsibilities seriously

What Makes a Virgo Tick?

Virgos are driven by the search for perfection in every way. This quest is apparent in everything they do or say—and especially in what they don't (or won't) do or say. In fact, they would rather do nothing than do the wrong thing, which often leads others to misinterpret their behavior as procrastination. But at the heart of the typical Virgo is the hardest worker you've ever met—ready, willing, and able to help anyone he deems worthy of his service.

The Virgo Personality Expressed Positively

Virgos who are driven to perform useful acts to the best of their abilities display the skillful, hardworking, and humble personality of their sign. Their ability to successfully solve any problem by paying close attention to the smallest of details is due to their ability to analyze people, situations, and procedures. They can analyze anything and devise a way to make it better.

On a Positive Note

Virgos displaying the positive characteristics associated with their sign also tend to be:

* gentle
* organized
* sympathetic
* humane
* high energy
* witty and charming
* knowledgeable about good health
* helpful
* dedicated

The Virgo Personality Expressed Negatively

Virgos who are unable to stop themselves from worrying about everyone and everything display the self-limiting tendency of their sign. They can get so bogged down attending to unimportant details that they miss the big picture. While they may express criticism with the best of intentions, this action can get them into trouble (and when their criticism is expressed with less-than-noble intentions, the ensuing trouble is that much greater).

Negative Traits

Virgos displaying the negative characteristics associated with their sign also tend to be:

* cranky and irritable
* dogmatic and harshly critical
* untidy
* hypochondriacal
* nervous and worried
* prudish
* overly demanding
* undemonstrative

Ask a Virgo If...

Ask a Virgo if you want to know the latest news and gossip, or if you want to know where to find the best of the best, from restaurants to theater. The importance that Virgos place on perfection leads them to seek out the crème de la crème in all sorts of areas in life. Their taste in all things is legendary, and if they are not artists or craftspeople themselves, they make good, though sometimes harsh, critics.

Virgos As Friends

Some of the best qualities possessed by Virgos are kindness, honesty, and a strong sense of responsibility. So it's not surprising that they tend to make great friends. And they can be extremely helpful friends to have, as Virgos need the opportunity to be useful to others and are at their best if they are allowed to take charge of as many apparently mundane matters as you can throw at them.

When it comes to making friends, Virgos are usually drawn to people who are tidy, clean, and intelligent. What's more, they tend to appreciate those who have a broad range of interests. Virgos tend to stay away from individuals given to big shows of emotion, preferring instead to spend time with those who offer a sense of peace and serenity.

Looking for Love

Virgos' quest for perfection extends to their love lives as well. The typical Virgo not only wants her partner to be perfect, but sets this benchmark for the way in which they get together, too. This can lead to wonderful, romantic interludes with fascinating people, but it can also lead to endless lonely nights if Virgos allow their impossibly high standards to prevent them from getting to know someone. Indeed, Virgos tend to be extremely picky about whom they get close to physically and emotionally. It is common to find a Virgo spending long periods without a love interest, but then suddenly moving in with someone who has passed all the tests she can throw at him.

Setting a high mark for others, however, is not the biggest obstacle Virgos face in finding a soul mate, nor is a fear of intimacy. Rather, the biggest stumbling block on Virgo's path to true love is the fear that once she has let a love interest get close, that person will discover that she is not perfect and will ultimately leave.

The way for a Virgo to keep a romantic relationship on track is not only to be aware of this tendency in herself, but to share it with a potential partner if it starts to become a problem. The good news is that this particular worry of Virgos is often found to be quite endearing by those who fall in love with them.

Finding That Special Someone

As Virgos tend to be discriminating, displaying a fine artistic taste and a wealth of knowledge on many subjects, museums, lectures, classes, food or wine tastings, galleries, concerts, and even libraries are the kinds of venues where Virgos can be at their best and ready to meet others.

First Dates

Virgos love pageantry. What's more, they delight in companions who share this love of fanfare. An ideal night out might involve tickets to the opera, with dinner at a restaurant known for its decor as well as its menu. Virgos like tasting-size portions and are usually delighted to order a number of small dishes so that a variety of intriguing delicacies may be sampled. After the evening is over, a Virgo remembers every costume and set change in the opera and is happy to recount them—as well as what she and her date wore, said, and did (and why)—in detail to friends.

Virgo in Love

Virgo is the most practical romantic in the zodiac. He is shy and slow to love because self-doubt and low self-esteem make him resistant to believing that someone could love him—even when that person genuinely thinks he's the best thing she's ever encountered. Though logical and analytical, a Virgo is not interested in anything less than the kind of true love found in fairy tales. When he falls in love, he will love intensely.

Undying Love

Forget one-night stands—they are all too often highly forgettable. Virgos are better off looking for a life of quality and meaning spent with a person to whom they are proud to be both a soul mate and a helpmate. Once they find love, their feelings will grow warmly and steadily, along with their devotion to their partner. What's more, having finally decided that a person is worthy of their affections, Virgos, characteristically shy and gentle, can demonstrate an almost volcanic passion that can become a central force in their formerly all-work-and-no-play lives.

Expectations in Love

Virgos expect the same 100 percent level of devotion from a committed partner that they themselves are always striving to give. But not everyone is capable of demonstrating such devotion, so Virgos can become disappointed in their partners for not reciprocating at an equal level and, as a result, can start to question the imbalance in the relationship. However, once Virgos accept that this is simply the way things are—that they are able to give much more than others can—they can return to giving 100 percent without reservation.

Virgos have a highly developed sense of decency and loyalty that they expect their partners to respect and emulate. Most are so committed to doing right by their partners that they are highly resistant to the charms of others and will never stray.

Virgos expect to be fussed over by their partners when they are feeling down. They also expect their personal matters, especially their faults and failings, to be kept private. Last but not least, they expect their feelings to be handled with tender loving care.

What Virgos Look For

Virgos are not looking for someone to cater to their every whim, nor are they likely to be dazzled by sexy makeup and clothes. Obvious good looks are not what attracts them to a potential partner; rather, it's what lies beneath the surface that matters to them. They appreciate a stellar person whose invaluable, wonderful qualities may be known only by them. This can sometimes lead friends and family to be confounded by their choice of partners.

If Virgos Only Knew...

If Virgos only knew the high regard others hold them in, they would realize that, as imperfect as they consider themselves to be, they're a lot closer to perfection than the rest of us! Those lucky enough to have a Virgo love interest are usually those seeking the best that life has to offer, which is why it is not unusual for two Virgos to get together; such a union is a unique experience for the rest of the world to observe, but it's not that unusual an occurrence.

Marriage

True to their analytical nature, Virgos approach a marriage proposal with great caution, weighing the pros and cons thoroughly before popping the question or giving an answer. While this behavior may sound cold and clinical, Virgos approach important life decisions in a methodical, thoughtful manner.

Those involved with a Virgo cannot expect a miraculous transformation after engagement or marriage. If anything, once Virgos are comfortable and secure in a relationship, they make an even greater effort to be perfect—as a tribute to their love.

A Virgo marriage ceremony will be either an affair worthy of magazine coverage or an elopement—nothing in between. Either every last detail will be made as perfect as possible or the pageantry will be dispensed with entirely, thereby saving the sanity of both parties.

Virgo's Opposite Sign

Pisces is the opposite sign of Virgo. A relationship between Virgo and Pisces can be difficult, but there are certain things that Virgo can learn from Pisces. Pisces can teach Virgo to accept help from another individual instead of giving all the time. Pisces can also show Virgo how to relax that inner critical voice a little and flow with the tide, giving her imagination a chance to develop. In this way, Virgo can begin to accept human imperfections, especially her own.

Pairing Up

In general, if people display the characteristics typical of their sign, intimate relationships between a Virgo and another individual can be described as follows:

Virgo with Virgo:	Harmonious; the quest for perfection shared!
Virgo with Libra:	Harmonious; such different types, but the relationship works
Virgo with Scorpio:	Harmonious, as long as the Scorpio is boss
Virgo with Sagittarius:	Difficult because respect is lacking
Virgo with Capricorn:	Harmonious, with both partners contributing to make it work
Virgo with Aquarius:	Difficult, filled with arguments that neither lover hears
Virgo with Pisces:	Harmonious because opposites attract, but then what?
Virgo with Aries:	Turbulent as lovers, but good as friends
Virgo with Taurus:	Harmonious and secure—first class!
Virgo with Gemini:	Difficult; Virgo practicality versus Gemini theories and fancies
Virgo with Cancer:	Harmonious; a true partnership of caring individuals
Virgo with Leo:	Harmonious; oh so different, yet the relationship can work!

If Things Don't Work Out

Virgos are typically loyal and will avoid ending a marriage or other permanent relationship whenever possible. However, in the long run, Virgos are sensible, practical people. If Virgo's sense of fair play has been outraged, he will make a quick and final break. Since a Virgo usually has good self-discipline, the past is soon put aside in favor of moving on to a new chapter.

Virgo at Work

A whole book could be written just about Virgos and work because they love it and are so good at it. Even the most career-oriented Virgo takes it one job at a time, a trait that gets her noticed by superiors as the go-to person in every situation. Unfortunately, this characteristic sometimes makes it hard for Virgos to advance to better jobs because they are seen as being essential to the job they already have. Their tendency to be humble often adds to this drag on their career and must be addressed, especially if the goal is to climb the corporate ladder.

Virgos' shrewd use of logic and incisive understanding, coupled with their ability to communicate their insights well, makes them essential to the success of enterprises large and small. They are the soul of efficiency and can analyze any system, laying bare its strengths and weaknesses and allowing a better system to be created. Their strength of character will not let them leave a project before it is finished, so if you ask them for help, let them help and don't expect them to stop until they think the job is finished.

To most Virgos, career plans and the expansion of existing projects are not as interesting as the details of everything they are already committed to. Virgos believe that every little job that they're involved with is equally important to their overall career. Although others might be able to get away with ignoring such matters, it is important for Virgos to pay special attention to pleasantries and minor rules and regulations. It is also important that they pay close attention to the precise meanings of words used in speech and writing, as well as the interpretation of policies.

Typical Occupations

A Virgo is well suited for any occupation that enables him to give service and handle complicated or difficult details. Health care, chemistry, pharmacology, engineering, accounting, programming, and architecture come to mind immediately, but there are many other careers where Virgo's precise manner and keen eye can come in handy. Quality control is a field where the sign's skill set can be put to especially good use. And arts that require masterful eye-hand coordination will provide much pleasure.

Really, Virgos can excel at virtually any pursuit they put their mind to, as long as it involves creative analysis rather than long-term business goals. The best type of job for Virgos involves breaking things down into their component parts and analyzing them.

Behavior and Abilities at Work

In the workplace, a typical Virgo:

* keeps everyone focused on details
* helps people in trouble or who ask for assistance
* displays meticulousness and self-discipline
* gives others a sense of stability
* enjoys complicated, routine tasks

Virgo As Employer

A typical Virgo boss:

* practices full disclosure
* demonstrates good manners
* remembers everything
* expects fairness from others
* expects good grooming and good habits
* handles complicated projects with aplomb

- rewards good work with pay, not perks
- leads by consensus

Virgo As Employee

A typical Virgo employee:

- has an inquiring, logical mind
- possesses excellent research and writing skills
- expects to be paid well
- demonstrates courtesy, reliability, and thoroughness
- works in a cautious, critical, and methodical fashion

Virgo As Coworker

Virgos take their professional relationships seriously, combining duty with devotion. Loyal and committed, they tend to develop the kind of bonds with coworkers that are more often found among family members.

Details, Details

Virgo is detail oriented and will make lists of things to do, executing them one by one. She remembers dates and agreements to the letter. She can be a wizard when it comes to the sensible balancing of the budget. She loves her work, honors her commitments, and criticizes everything—to make it better, of course.

Virgo is shy but as tough as nails when the need arises. In business, she is cool, intelligent, and fully committed. Virgos often meet their romantic partners through their job or profession. They feel more like themselves when they are fully engaged in their work than at practically any other time.

Of all the signs, Virgos are the most adept at suppressing their feelings and emotions for fear that they may be seen as weak. They are thus quick to criticize decisions based purely on "gut instinct," preferring logical analysis instead. For this reason, a Virgo is best off working with individuals who are able to counter the Virgo's point of view with gentle but forceful insistence that intuition is the complement to logic, not its antithesis.

Money

Virgos have the ability to attain any reward they work for diligently and patiently. Being practical ensures that Virgos have enough when they need it the most. Fortunately, Virgos do not succumb to the temptation of immediate gratification. And while they tend to wait until they can afford the best, they won't break themselves to do so. Virgos save their resources for the future. These resources are not always money or wealth in the material sense, though they often are. What Virgos consider necessary for their own success is what is important. These necessities can take the form of family connections, friendships, favors owed, and even secrets shared. The strength of their faith, in terms of religion and what they are committed to, is as important as any material resource.

At Home

Virgos thrive at home, as they are the most relaxed in their own space. They prefer to putter around, fixing, tidying, and tending to household chores, rather than being out and about. They are usually either compulsively neat or total slobs. Virgos often have prized collections of things, sometimes things others might consider odd things to collect.

Behavior and Abilities at Home

Virgo typically:

* enjoys planning and fixing
* is adept in such areas as cooking, management of general maintenance, and gardening
* likes to be doing or making something instead of sitting around idly
* pursues several hobbies at or from home

Leisure Interests

Most Virgos enjoy engaging in intellectual pursuits and hands-on hobbies during their free time. Restless by nature, they need plenty of activities to keep them occupied. They are not, however, naturally inclined toward sports, though many exercise regularly for the sake of their health.

The typical Virgo enjoys the following pastimes:

* playing with the latest high-tech gadgets
* attending concerts and plays
* gardening
* reading books and magazines
* creating detailed craft projects
* engaging in needlework or model making
* taking self-improvement courses

Virgoan Likes

* lists and plans and punctuality
* nice soaps
* small animals
* flowers and herbs
* name brands of high quality
* healthy foods
* beautiful serving plates
* interesting collections
* ingenious storage bins and boxes
* muted colors

Virgoan Dislikes

* crowds, noise, and brash people
* slang and cursing

- dirt and disorder
- people who complain a lot
- sitting still for a long time
- disrupted routines
- lids left off boxes, or tops off toothpaste
- being obligated to others
- having their personal things moved by others
- bright, bold, primary colors

The Secret Side of Virgo

Inside anyone who has strong Virgo influences is a tendency to worry too much about every personal imperfection and to never be satisfied with her own standards. A Virgo may appear on the surface to be a know-it-all and a compulsive worker, but these aspects of her personality mask a deep fear that she is not good enough, especially for her job or her partner.

Mercury

Mercury, the planet of the mind and communication, rules the sign of Virgo, so those born under this sign are mentally quick, incisive, and sharp. Drawn to education—both teaching and learning—Virgos are particularly interested in computers.

Thanks to Mercury's strong association with communication (in Roman mythology, the god Mercury was known as the "winged messenger"), Virgos are good at keeping in touch. Great correspondents, they enjoy sending letters and e-mail. What's more, they're witty and wonderful conversationalists, able to recount and act out whole scenarios and events in detail.

Bringing Up a Young Virgo

Young Virgos need plenty of hugs and sincere compliments every day to build self-confidence—a trait that Virgos typically are not born with. Young

Virgos try very hard to please, as long as they know clearly what is expected of them.

As they grow up, Virgos often find close relationships with the opposite sex challenging. Offering them much genuine praise and encouragement early in life will help to smooth the path to true love in the teenage years and early adulthood. It takes a lot of convincing to make Virgos believe they are physically attractive people and worthy of love, as they are extremely self-critical.

On the whole, young Virgos strive for good grades at school and help out around the house. Exacting about time, food, and orderliness, they tend to be extremely neat, almost to a fault, when it comes to their belongings. An untidy Virgo will have some other strong influence countering her Sun sign in her astrological birth chart.

Virgo children have a tendency to be critical about everyone else in the family, especially when asked for an opinion. They therefore need to be taught to accept other people's foibles and not to get upset about little things that aren't important.

The Virgo Child

The typical Virgo child:

- is quick and alert
- is an excellent mimic
- can learn many things in a short time
- is often an early talker and reader
- gets upset if she forgets something that she previously memorized
- rarely questions authority
- frequently questions facts

* is honest and reliable
* demonstrates shyness with strangers
* loves to do jobs around the home, imitating an adult
* can be a fussy eater
* tends to be tidy, with occasional bouts of disorganization
* gets very upset if teased

Virgo As a Parent

The typical Virgo parent:

* encourages children to ask questions
* supports practical activities during free time
* worries about the children's health
* may find it hard to express affection warmly
* gets upset by children's dirt and untidiness
* explains the demands he makes
* does anything to help his children

Health

Virgos are typically healthy and usually take good care of themselves. However, if terribly worried or unhappy, they may succumb to their sign's tendency toward hypochondria.

Virgos can experience frequent stomachaches stemming from their anxious, nervous nature. To maintain their health, they should be wary of working too much and instead learn to relax. However, Virgos often have to trick themselves into relaxing by thinking of it as one more job on their long to-do list. They should sleep more, and spend as much time as possible walking outdoors. Virgos should also avoid alcohol and foods that are very spicy.

FAMOUS VIRGOS

Fiona Apple

Lauren Bacall

Leonard Bernstein

Andrea Bocelli

Sean Connery

Cameron Diaz

Greta Garbo

Richard Gere

Faith Hill

Michael Jackson

Jesse James

Lyndon B. Johnson

B.B. King

Stephen King

Sophia Loren

Marlee Matlin

Bill Murray

Bob Newhart

Otis Redding

Keanu Reeves

Jada Pinkett Smith

Mother Teresa

Lily Tomlin

Twiggy

Luke Wilson

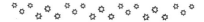

LIBRA
September 23–October 22

LIBRA
September 23–October 22

Planet: Venus
Element: Air
Quality: Cardinal
Day: Friday
Season: autumn
Colors: light blue, royal blue, pastels
Plants: orchid, foxglove, eucalyptus
Perfume: vanilla
Gemstones: opal, jade, sapphire, blue topaz
Metal: copper
Personal qualities: Artistic, refined, poised, intelligent, and tactful

Keywords

We call the following words "keywords" because they can help you unlock the core meaning of the astrological sign of Libra. Each keyword represents issues and ideas that are of supreme importance and prominence in the lives of people born with Libra as their Sun sign. You will usually find that every Libra embodies at least one of these keywords in the way she makes a living:

partnership • union • color sense • sophistication • good taste
yin and yang • law • balance • cooperation • fairness
quality control • detachment • aesthetics • harmonious
fence-sitter • romantic • ideas • opinions • politics • diplomacy

good manners • fashionista • give peace a chance • moderate
pro and con • mellifluous • idealism • comfort • shopping • justice

Libra's Symbolic Meaning

Libra is the only sign whose symbol is not alive, not a human, animal, or fish. Its symbol is the old-fashioned balance scale, a representation of equal measure and justice. The scales of Libra remind us that the time of Libra was when the harvest was weighed and measured against those of other years and other farmers. Public declarations of contractual partnerships were made and fulfilled, as goods were exchanged for their fair market value. But the perfect balance of the Libran scales was also a reminder that the first six warming full Moons of the lunar year had passed and that the challenges of the next six cooling full Moons were to come. Our ancestors knew that a balanced, loving relationship was a truly valuable commodity on cold nights. Only a cooperative family unit could make it through winter's deprivations.

Libra is one of the four Cardinal Sun signs in astrology (the other three are Aries, Cancer, and Capricorn). Cardinal people like to initiate change, as each Cardinal sign represents the beginning of a new season. Consequently, they like to take charge, and they take action to direct and control.

Libra is also one of the three Air signs of astrology (the other two are Gemini and Aquarius). The Air signs are usually connected with communication and the intellect.

The lesson for all Libras to learn is that there is an important reason that their judgment is not as refined, elegant, and accurate as they would like it to be. They have come into this world with the astrological sign Libra because they want to learn how to develop their judgment and become the best competitor for the finer things in life. Libras hate anything they consider not up to their standards and want to be surrounded by only the best. Perhaps this is why Libras are such an interesting mixture of refined judgment and fierce competitiveness.

Libras too often allow themselves to be persuaded to abandon their own judgment and distrust their intuition. The scales that symbolize Libra are an inanimate device intended to indicate the relative weight or value of everything by attaining a position of rest, resolution, and harmony. A scale never brought to a state of equilibrium is almost worthless. Libras have a natural affinity with the unseen, intuitive side of life. With the exceedingly rare and keen perception characteristic of the sign Libra, there is no human attainment beyond their grasp.

Recognizing a Libra

People who exhibit the physical characteristics distinctive of the sign Libra have a fine bone structure and balanced features, a charming smile, a graceful and athletic build, and a clear and very harmonious voice. Libras are likely to have an attractive dimple. It is a Libran habit to spend time deciding what to wear each morning, and he knows how to dress in gentle, subtle colors.

Libra's Typical Behavior and Personality Traits

- has a hard time making decisions
- enjoys beautiful art and music
- is a great conversationalist
- is interested in the opposite sex
- knows how to be romantic
- is amusing and smiles a lot
- is very idealistic
- can change his mind often
- can spend a lot of money on luxury items
- has good business instincts
- has good manners
- is interested in legal matters

What Makes a Libra Tick?

Libras are driven by the desire to bring beauty and harmony to their world and the world at large. They have refined tastes and may actually recoil from things that are ugly, loud, or unpleasant. Other people may misinterpret this attitude as snobbishness, but it is not. For many Libras, vulgarity is an affront.

A Libra may give the impression of being a pushover because of an unwillingness to argue. But under the right set of circumstances he can stand up for himself, despite the unpleasantness that arguing brings.

The Libra Personality Expressed Positively

Libras who use their talent for mediating disputes in their daily life are acting out their own innate sense of harmony, and they manage to do this without appearing to be nosy or intrusive. They have a genuine desire for peace and equality in every relationship, and when they are happy these attributes are easily attained and flow through their actions.

On a Positive Note

Libras displaying the positive characteristics associated with their sign also tend to be:

* cooperative and trustworthy
* excellent companions
* refined and artistic
* idealistic and romantic
* good negotiators
* fair-minded
* strong believers in good causes
* planners
* charming and sincere

The Libra Personality Expressed Negatively

An unhappy or frustrated Libra can be hard to get along with and deliberately quarrelsome. If Libra feels that she is lacking in power, she can do a lot of moping and self-pitying. Also, if Libra doesn't get enough attention, the result is likely to be a lowering of confidence and self-esteem. Libra needs to shine in someone else's eyes, and unless she does, she cannot be at her best.

Negative Traits

Libras displaying the negative characteristics associated with their sign also tend to be:

* fearful
* lazy and indecisive
* manipulative
* know-it-all
* flirtatious
* narcissistic
* jealous
* depressed

Ask a Libra If...

Ask a Libra if you want to see both sides of a difficult or troublesome situation. Libras are notoriously good at being able to size up any situation and discover the pluses and minuses of it. Libra isn't merely content to analyze the available options, but actually believes that there are two sides to every story. Even if a Libra has a preference for one or the other, he will be fair in making an assessment.

Libras As Friends

Libras are loving friends and are unlikely to embarrass anyone with emotional outbursts. Libran friends are honest and treat their friends fairly. They need to keep a balance between work and play, and between their thoughts and their emotions. This is what makes them happy. Friends should never forget that the worst thing for a Libra is to be left alone for too long. If this happens, Libras can become irritable and depressed, and their self-esteem can suffer. Friends also need to know that Libras find it difficult to ask for help when they are feeling unhappy.

Sometimes Libras seem to have trouble making decisions, but this is because they must consider all sides of a question first. Libras can occasionally try the patience of their friends with their indecisiveness.

Libras are always striving for perfection, and need beauty and balance around them. The most important thing for a Libra person is the idea of harmony.

Looking for Love

Libras are very partner oriented and often find it difficult to function efficiently without one. It's not that they depend upon their partner for much. Libras need a partner so they can find out what they, themselves, think about something by bouncing it off of another person. When they find a partner who, in this way, enables them to feel the way they want to feel, they seek to make the partnership permanent. This often leads to partnerships that others have difficulty understanding. It also makes Libras very concerned with living up to the conditions of partnerships. Libras love to be in love.

Libras need good communication with others. The smooth-talking socialites of the zodiac, Libras are happy to flatter, to console, and to make their love interests feel comfortable. But that is not to say that they desire insincere flattery. They are extremely intelligent and can always tell if someone is being honest or merely trying to get on their good side. Libras want harmony above all else but will not be falsely placated just to achieve the semblance of it. They're also very considerate of a loved one's needs and always try to see things from their mate's point of view.

Even though Libras are not intellectual snobs, they do look for someone who is full of ideas and opinions and with whom they can have rousing discussions. There are times when even romantic infatuation or attraction isn't enough—Libra needs the words!

Finding That Special Someone

As Libras are extremely sociable, they have no problem meeting interesting people. Because their talent for conversation makes them interesting dinner party guests, they have more than their share of invitations. Since they have so many friends, it is not uncommon for Libras to be introduced to a potential love interest by mutual friends.

First Dates

A first date with a Libra usually involves some classy event where an attractive new outfit is required. Most Libras love the arts and parties. An ideal first date would be to any gathering where there was a mix of interesting people. Libras love good food but are often watching their weight, so the appetizers and wine served at such an event may be enough for them. Afterwards, though, they may choose to have a cup of coffee at a trendy place to discuss the evening's events. For Libra, the talk may even prove to be the best part of the date.

Libra in Love

The Libra can glow with love for the whole world when she meets the person of her dreams. She tends to fall in love with love itself and is eager to share life, with all its ups and downs, with her partner. The Libran ideal is a life that is filled with the gentle, peaceful, rosy glow of romance. She will do anything to avoid hurting her loved one, and can become extremely emotionally dependent on her partner.

Undying Love

The Libra is able to forgive a lot of his loved one's shortcomings. A loved one can lighten Libra's depressive moods with a genuine loving gesture. A Libra may argue or behave badly when he feels that something is unfair.

Libras are not nearly as high maintenance as they may appear. Because they are so reasonable, it is easy to talk to them about concerns in the relationship without them becoming aggravated or overly emotional. They are always willing to do their part in keeping the relationship not only working but improving.

Expectations in Love

The sign of Libra is one of the most positive for relationships, both romantic and committed partnerships of all kinds. If a Libra is in a relationship, he needs to be supported and cared for as well as admired and even exalted.

If a relationship is new, a Libra should make sure his partner is someone whom he likes a lot and who is willing to wait awhile before moving the relationship to the physical stage. When a Libra finds that person, you can rest assured that a wonderful time in his life is at hand and that his fabulous love life will be with someone positive whom he loves and trusts. Faithfulness and loyalty are essential to a Libra.

A Libra also needs a partner to have her own separate interests, as it is important to him to be free to get on with his work.

What Libras Look For

While Libras have a reputation for being attracted only to good-looking people, they are really looking for much more. They appreciate someone who is intelligent and has a pleasing personality. Most of all, they are dazzled by a person who can hold his own in conversational banter. While they are happiest when they can find someone who has all of these attributes, brains will always win out over looks with the clever people of this sign.

If Libras Only Knew

If Libras only knew that any trouble in a relationship with a Libra will come from one or both partners not fulfilling their obligations with honesty and a giving heart. Libra may have learned from others whom she looked up to and respected that this unequal and disappointing tendency was the way to act in a relationship. Libras believe deeply in the power of communication in any relationship. They feel that issues, good and bad, can be handled and solved as long as the talking doesn't stop.

Marriage

The person who partners Libra can expect the marriage to be happy and successful. Libra is the zodiac sign of partnerships, and typical Libras cannot imagine life without a relationship. A Libra will work hard and thoughtfully to make the partnership a harmonious balance of two personalities, but she needs plenty of encouragement.

The person who contemplates becoming the marriage partner of a typical Libra must realize that Libra forms partnerships to escape the loneliness that is always present inside her heart.

Libra wants a partner who has some good business or social connections, too. Libra has plenty of talent and energy and is ambitious to be successful in her marriage, business, and social life.

In a partnership, Libra generally takes charge of the financial planning, making sure that there is always a good bank balance.

Libra's Opposite Sign

The opposite sign of Libra is Aries. Although relationships between them can be difficult, they can also become extremely complementary. From Aries, Libra can learn to take the initiative and stand up for his beliefs. Libra can also learn from Aries how to become self-sufficient and how to gain a greater sense of personal identity, apart from his partner. In this way, Libra, the sign of partnership, may be able to enjoy a separate identity while in a partnership.

Pairing Up

In general, if people display the characteristics typical of their sign, intimate relationships between a Libra and another individual can be described as follows:

Libra with Libra:	Harmonious; a meeting of minds, spirits, and hearts
Libra with Scorpio:	Harmonious, if Scorpio can treat Libra with sensitivity
Libra with Sagittarius:	Harmonious, since they are best friends as well as lovers
Libra with Capricorn:	Difficult, because both signs are stubborn
Libra with Aquarius:	Harmonious; true soul mates forever
Libra with Pisces:	Turbulent, unless Pisces can learn not to lean on Libra
Libra with Aries:	Difficult, yet each can learn a lot from the other
Libra with Taurus:	Turbulent, with a lot of bickering and passion
Libra with Gemini:	Harmonious; a joyful, fascinating love match
Libra with Cancer:	Difficult, yet enriched by shared values
Libra with Leo:	Harmonious, since both partners are equally romantic
Libra with Virgo:	Harmonious, so long as financial matters are handled with care

If Things Don't Work Out

Because of their dedication to a life partnership, Libras don't like to end a relationship. Not only is there the feeling of disappointment for a dream that has faded, but there is also the prospect of being alone. Libras are not happy alone, so ending a relationship takes a great deal of courage on their part. Thankfully, most of them have the good sense and self-confidence to prefer living solo to staying in a relationship that no longer works as a positive force in their life.

Libra at Work

Libras work very hard to attain the goal of resolving conflict, either through compromise and diplomacy or by fighting the good fight if they are forced to. They are constantly trying to balance the scales of justice regarding practically everything, and that can be very trying, not only personally but also for others. Their desire to make the perfect decision can sometimes prevent them from acting decisively until it is too late to do so. A Libra can be a bit bossy but uses charm and reasoning to convince people of the value of her side of an issue. Libras find it easy to associate and work with others. At work they can serve as good managers, counselors, and collaborators.

People often misread Libra's amiable personality for reticence or weakness, but this is not the case. Anyone who has ever gone up against Libra in a power play knows that she is not only determined but also extremely well versed in the art of arguing a point of view. Libras don't like being manipulated and are unlikely to stoop to this tactic themselves. But they do have the ability to defuse a challenger's argument with wit and charm. For the most part, they get along famously with others.

Typical Occupations

Libras are liable to be involved with any aspect of the law, politics, or diplomacy. Their eye for design may lead them into areas such as fashion, interior decoration, art dealership, and graphics. Naturally creative and artistic, some Libras are gifted fine artists, composers, and musicians. Others may find success as critics, writers, or managers in various areas of entertainment. They also enjoy working in jobs that involve talking and presentation, such as promotional work. Many Libras are good at planning business ventures. Finance is also a fair field, as Libras are trustworthy in handling other people's money.

In a profession or business, Libras often succeed as administrators, lawyers, doctors, antique dealers, or civil servants. Those with a gift for finance sometimes make good speculators, for they have the optimism and ability to recover from financial setbacks.

It is a good idea for a Libra to be doing work that involves interaction with the public or coworkers. Jobs that work best could involve publicity, negotiations, and working in the support industries that service weddings and parties.

Behavior and Abilities at Work

In the workplace, a typical Libra:

* is a great resource for ideas
* knows how to compromise
* likes to make contracts
* builds a good network of contacts
* takes time to do things properly
* looks for ways to advance her career

Libra As Employer

A typical Libra boss:

* doesn't like to be pushed too far
* is an extremely good analyst
* takes everyone's opinion into consideration

- suggests that she is an expert
- can argue both sides of an issue
- has a strong opinion about neatness
- is financially savvy

Libra As Employee

A typical Libra employee:

- makes good presentations
- has good manners
- is an effective mediator
- can be moody at times
- expects and gives a fair deal
- belongs to an organization
- needs a long vacation
- dresses well and appropriately

Libra As Coworker

Sometimes, fearful of discord, Libras become paralyzed with indecision. They easily see the value of another person's point of view. But often, if they do not hold a definite opinion of their own, they fail to take a stand. If they lose confidence in their own views and try to reconcile them with what others may think, they can become confused, vulnerable, and aggressive.

Details, Details

When it comes to life's day-to-day details, Libras have the ability to handle them with ease. But that doesn't mean they always do. They sometimes overlook details, especially if they involve suffering or cannot be resolved elegantly.

They need to fulfill their part of all agreements, rules, and regulations. A Libra must find a way that he can work with others without feeling that he has had to still his own unique voice to do it. Because this isn't always easy for him, he can become frustrated and unnecessarily argumentative. Similarly, working within time constraints or a budget can frazzle him and stifle his creative instincts.

In their continual search for balance, Libras strive to see both sides, even when that turns out to be an exercise in futility. Sometimes just for argument's sake they take an opposing viewpoint. This is their way of familiarizing themselves with all the possible details involved in a project or endeavor. But while it is important for a Libra to be acquainted with this information, he actually works much better as the "idea person," delegating the detail-oriented work to others.

Money

If Libras are uncommunicative about any area of their life, that area is likely to be money. They usually handle their financial affairs with discretion, preferring to keep such things to themselves. It is also typical for Libras to refrain from telling people how much they spent for a particular item, since to them, it sounds like bragging.

Libras have the ability to be practical about money, but that doesn't mean that they always succeed. They have very extravagant tastes and can find it hard to live on a budget. Immediate gratification can be a problem for them, since when they see something beautiful they want to own it.

Beauty is as important to Libras as money, so if they are surrounded by beautiful things they count themselves wealthy. The best of them measure success by the harmonious elements working in their lives, not by how much money they have in the bank.

At Home

If an individual has the personality that is typical of those born with a Libra Sun sign, home is a place to retire to for rest and recuperation, to prepare for the next period of sustained activity.

Librans find home the one place where it is difficult for them to compromise. They simply have to have things their way, especially when it comes to their home's appearance, design, and decoration.

Behavior and Abilities at Home

Libra typically:

* uses good taste to make the decor beautiful
* offers good food and wines to guests
* keeps the home clean and tidy
* spends time just lounging around
* creates a healing environment
* makes a very gracious host
* takes an active role in redecorating

Leisure Interests

A Libra loves a luxurious home where she can be totally lazy. While at rest, the Libran mind is rarely still, always planning ahead, and at times that is enough activity for her. She likes to have sensual bed linens and sophisticated colors surrounding her.

The typical Libra enjoys the following pastimes:

* listening to music
* reading poetry
* dancing classes
* spending time in romantic settings
* shopping for fashion
* gourmet cooking
* interior design as a hobby
* going to parties

Libra Likes

* getting flowers
* having friends around
* working with a partner
* well-made, expensive clothes
* a stimulating discussion
* planning a party
* having help
* attending to the finest details
* beautiful surroundings
* soft color schemes
* being admired

Libra Dislikes

* injustice
* disharmony
* sloppiness
* arguing in public
* ugly clothes
* having to make big decisions
* being alone
* bad manners
* taking out the garbage
* vulgarity

The Secret Side of Libra

Inside any Libra is a person who is terrified of being alone. The fear is usually well controlled, so the typical Libra always looks calm, collected, and in charge of any situation.

Good-natured and loving, Libras can also be petulant, and even objectionable, when asked to take orders. Similarly, they are extremely intelligent, yet sometimes gullible; they enjoy talking to people, yet can also be very attentive listeners. Although they believe in equality, they sometimes yearn to be subservient to their partners.

Venus

Venus is the planet of romantic love, beauty, and the arts that are associated with them. Sociable Venus rules over parties and pleasurable meetings. She accomplishes her goals by attracting only what she wants and rejecting the rest, thus making taste and values two of her special talents. Diplomacy, tact, and gentleness are a few of the arts that are ruled by Venus.

The love and beauty that Venus represents have the power to both unite and heal, and a more desirable and powerful combination is difficult to imagine. Venus rules our senses of touch, taste, and smell—everything must achieve harmony before usefulness.

Bringing Up a Young Libra

Most young Libras learn quickly how to argue about everything with total conviction. At a very early age young Libra needs to be given direction and told, gently and firmly, what to do and when to do it. Little Libra uses this natural ability to make his needs and wants known. Parents needs to take an optimistic view of this tendency and should provide plenty of sound information. Young Libra absorbs information readily from books. What may appear to be reluctance to do something is often a sign that young Libra is giving extensive thought to the matter at hand.

While young Libras can pursue their interests alone, they also need company. It is from bonding with others that they learn who they really are. It is never a good idea to scold little Libras too much, especially in front of others. Doing so makes them feel ashamed and embarrassed. It could also make them feel that if they are going to fail, it had better not be in front of parents or other authority figures.

A harmonious environment and fair treatment are essential to the developing Libra. Privacy is regarded as sacred. Similarly, young Libra respects the privacy of others and keeps confidences. Affection is crucial.

The Libra Child

The typical Libra child:

* hates having to decide between two things
* does not like to be hurried
* has a naturally sweet temperament
* always seems mature for her age
* likes to be fair and to be treated fairly
* can charm her friends and parents
* obeys rules if they make sense
* loves bubble baths
* likes candy and desserts
* shares toys with other children
* is usually neat and clean
* is kindhearted

Libra As a Parent

The typical Libra parent:

* tries to be just and fair
* may spoil the children
* shows much affection
* gives children the best possible education
* will probably dominate the family
* encourages artistic pursuits

- likes kids to be neat and well dressed
- stresses manners and good behavior
- encourages a child's fantasy life

Health

Expecting a good life, Libras easily become depressed whenever difficulties arise and can suffer from severe headaches in their mental efforts to resolve problems. When Libras are unhappy, they tend to overeat. They are happier and healthier when engaged in rewarding work. It can also take a great deal of effort for them to motivate themselves to exercise regularly. Libras have a generally strong constitution, but their kidneys and bladder may let them down later in life due to their fondness for wining and dining.

Libra rules the adrenals, kidneys, skin, and lumbar nerves. Diseases such as kidney and bladder disorders, or eczema and skin diseases, can be a problem.

FAMOUS LIBRAS

Julie Andrews

Lorraine Bracco

Truman Capote

Catherine Deneuve

Michael Douglas

F. Scott Fitzgerald

George Gershwin

Rita Hayworth

Charlton Heston

Jesse Jackson

Ralph Lauren

John Lennon

Franz Liszt

Mickey Mantle

Eugene O'Neill

Gwyneth Paltrow

Luciano Pavarotti

Christopher Reeve

Anne Rice

Eleanor Roosevelt

Susan Sarandon

Paul Simon

Sting

Usher

Catherine Zeta-Jones

"Men should take their knowledge from the Sun, the Moon and the Stars."

—RALPH WALDO EMERSON

SCORPIO
October 23–November 21

SCORPIO
October 23–November 21

Planet: Pluto

Element: Water

Quality: Fixed

Day: Tuesday

Season: autumn

Colors: black, dark red, maroon

Plants: gardenia, rhododendron, anemone

Perfume: tuberose

Gemstones: agate, onyx, ruby, obsidian

Metal: plutonium

Personal qualities: Intense, obsessive, loyal, determined, and passionate

Keywords

We call the following words "keywords" because they can help you unlock the core meaning of the astrological sign of Scorpio. Each keyword represents issues and ideas that are of supreme importance and prominence in the lives of people born with Scorpio as their Sun sign. You will usually find that every Scorpio embodies at least one of these keywords in the way he makes a living.

investigation • wills and taxes • secrets • profundity • intuition
sexual politics • mysteries • good detective • transformation
power play • transcend • resurrect • legacy • regenerate

absolute • conscience • labyrinth • control • obsession • judge
purify • death and transfiguration • clues • precision • research
enemies list • subterfuge • underground tunnel • recycling
exchange • psychology • reincarnation

Scorpio's Symbolic Meaning

Scorpio is the master detective of the zodiac. If there's something or some-one Scorpio wants to know about, nothing and no one can prevent her from discovering the hidden truth. It is as if she feels compelled to know all the secrets just in case she needs to use them to prove how powerful she is.

When it comes to their own secrets, Scorpios are equally skilled at keep-ing them from others. In this way they prevent others from having power over them. They rarely volunteer information, for the same reason. Power in all its forms is one of the biggest issues for Scorpios to deal with. Most elements of life are imbued with overtones of power for Scorpio, including money, sex, authority, and knowledge. Most Scorpios are powerful and know it. However, if a Scorpio doubts her own power, she becomes so attracted to it that she is willing to do practically anything to get it. This can obviously put her in intense situations.

Most Scorpios are as fearless as their most well-known symbol, the Scorpion. But like a scorpion, they can be so intent on stinging something that they end up stinging themselves. Their intensity is such that other people can't believe that they really mean what they are saying. Scorpios are often misunderstood because of the intensity of their passion. The other symbol for this sign is the Phoenix, which rises in triumph from its own ashes. This archetype symbolizes the extremes to which the sign is typi-cally drawn.

Scorpio is one of the four Fixed Sun signs in astrology (the other three are Taurus, Aquarius, and Leo). Fixed signs are associated with stability and determination. Concentration, focus, consolidation, and perseverance are all hallmarks of a fixed Sun sign. Scorpio is the Fixed Water sign of the zodiac. It is one of three Water signs in the zodiac (the other two are Pisces and Cancer). Water is the element that makes a Scorpio emotional, sensitive, feeling, and hidden. In the case of Scorpio, still waters do run deep.

The lesson for Scorpios to learn is that there is an important reason that their life does not provide them with as many peak experiences as they would like. They have come into this world with the astrological sign Scorpio because they want to learn how to develop their ability to work their powerful will on the world. The sign Scorpio rules magic, and Scorpios want to make big changes in their lives, the kinds that appear to other people as almost magical transformations.

Recognizing a Scorpio

People who exhibit the physical characteristics distinctive of the sign of Scorpio have strong features, attractive looks, thick hair and eyebrows, and eyes with an almost hypnotic intensity. A Scorpio is inclined to point his head down. Even in repose, Scorpio's expression remains intense. When looking directly at a person, a Scorpio makes his subject feel penetrated. A Scorpio, even when slender, can have a rather thick waist.

Scorpio's Typical Behavior and Personality Traits

* is loyal to family and home
* is intensely loyal to friends
* is passionate about beliefs
* never forgives or forgets
* is relentless about winning
* flirts only when seriously interested
* has very high standards
* can be a saint or a sinner
* has to maintain his dignity

- is a force to be reckoned with
- is very brave under adversity
- gives ruthlessly honest advice
- pursues interests with great zeal
- can be quite secretive
- will work behind the scenes

What Makes a Scorpio Tick?

Scorpios are keen students of psychology and always want to know what makes people do the things they do. Compulsions and strange behavior do not faze a Scorpio one bit. In fact, her curiosity is piqued. Undeveloped Scorpios have a tendency to use their intimate understanding of human motivations for ruthless manipulation cunningly designed to attain selfish goals. While Scorpios are constantly trying to uncover the secrets of others, they guard their own privacy with almost manic intensity.

The Scorpio Personality Expressed Positively

It is in the nature of Scorpio to pursue an interest or endeavor to its limit, regardless of personal cost or effort. That is how a Scorpio best fulfills his destiny. This is a Sun sign of extremes, and Scorpio often takes his desire for secrecy very seriously, resulting in cordial yet careful relationships.

On a Positive Note

Scorpios displaying the positive characteristics associated with their sign also tend to be:

- protective of loved ones
- magnetic and dynamic
- compassionate and emotional
- tenacious and probing
- safety conscious

- passionate
- intense concentrators
- sensual
- intuitive

The Scorpio Personality Expressed Negatively

A frustrated Scorpio can be a difficult and angry person. Usually this is the result of feeling as if she has a lack of power or a sense that her life is not progressing in the way she hoped. Since it can be hard for an unhappy Scorpio to admit any fault, she has a tendency to blame others for her failures.

Negative Traits

Scorpios displaying the negative characteristics associated with their sign also tend to be:

- ruthless and vindictive
- jealous and possessive
- suspicious
- self-destructive
- intolerant and sarcastic
- obstinate
- secretive
- moody
- insulting

Ask a Scorpio If...

Ask a Scorpio if you want to get to the bottom of a mystery. Their penetrating intelligence and ability to put clues together are a tremendous help. Scorpios also have strong powers of intuition, which helps them to discover truths both minor and major. They are also great judges of character, so it is very hard to fool them in any way. If a Scorpio has advice to give, it is best to listen. They aren't gossips and aren't the sort who spread idle rumors. A Scorpio can carry a secret to his deathbed.

Scorpios As Friends

When Scorpios focus their energies on controlling their friends, they find in the end that they, themselves, end up being under the control of others. However, when they turn their efforts towards self-control, the influence they have on both their friends and the world around them seems to be without bounds. It is as if the best way for them to control a situation is to be in control of themselves.

In general, Scorpio likes a friend who recognizes Scorpio's magnetic and intense personality and appreciates that she is deeply caring and emotionally involved. Scorpio chooses only a few friends and expects loyalty from them. Scorpio keeps close friends for many years.

Scorpios have good memories and enjoy telling jokes. They are generous and hospitable toward friends, and also make strangers welcome when they call for help or advice.

Looking for Love

Despite their passionate nature and need to feel as if they are the center of someone's world, Scorpios do not fall in and out of love easily or often. Individuals born under the sign of Scorpio are very careful about the people they choose to become romantically involved with because they want a relationship that lasts. It is hard for them to be casual about any relationship. Scorpios set very high standards, and although they are not looking for perfection, they demand honesty, passion, and commitment.

Scorpios are known for being deeply sexual, but because they are often driven to extremes, a Scorpio may, for her own reasons, be celibate for long periods of time. Even though she is happiest when in a satisfying sexual relationship, she prefers being alone to having a series of one-night stands or short-term relationships.

When Scorpio does find the right person, she moves quickly. It may often seem to the people who know her that Scorpio moves too fast in a relationship, but this is very much in her nature. Scorpio is happiest when power, control, and passion all come together. For this reason she is likely to fall in love with someone whose temperament matches hers. This allows the power in a relationship to be balanced, and Scorpio will not be tempted to be the one who runs the relationship.

Finding That Special Someone

Surprisingly, Scorpios may not make a concerted effort to look for a soul mate. Although this sounds unlikely, it relates to their intuitive sense. They have a tendency to believe that true love and attraction are based on destiny, and that if they are meant to meet their true "other half," they will. For them, such meetings may happen at a library, bookstore, planetarium, charity event, or church.

First Dates

Scorpios prefer quiet, intimate venues, especially for something as important as a first date. Yet, because they are not particularly talkative, they may enjoy an atmosphere that is relaxing but does not demand constant conversation. The best choice is to surround them with music at a jazz club, rock concert, opera, or even a musical at a dinner theater. Scorpios' deep emotions are stirred by music in ways that words cannot touch. They are a Water sign, so an evening walk on the beach, or a sunset stroll by the lake puts them at ease.

Scorpio in Love

Scorpios are deeply attached to their loved ones. They can be possessive and dominating, but they are also very faithful when they are in love. They believe that fidelity is one of the most important elements in a relationship.

Scorpios aspire to a level of purity that is hard for the other Sun signs to even imagine. Scorpios attract their loved ones like a magnet, and have an almost psychic insight into the motives and secrets of their mates. Anyone who dislikes someone knowing their secrets should stay away from Scorpios.

Undying Love

They may be known as the sexiest sign, but there is absolutely nothing trivial or superficial about the way Scorpios approach love. They believe in sincerity and honesty. However, there is also a negative side to their intensity, which can sometimes lead them to be obsessed by their love for someone. Separation from the one she loves isn't only unpleasant; it is actually painful. It can be hard for a Scorpio to keep from being wildly jealous if she feels that someone is trying to steal the affections of the one she loves.

Expectations in Love

Scorpio expects passion and intensity and absolute faithfulness in her relationships. Although her love life may take on the appearance of a romance novel, this is how Scorpio likes it. She is very demonstrative, and makes her lover feel very special. She expects complete loyalty, and can be the most tender and passionate mate if she feels secure.

Scorpios often rush into having a sexual relationship before they have any other kind of relationship. This dangerous habit it is usually the result of a desire for approval. Because emotional intimacy is so important to them, they sometimes make themselves believe that physical intimacy will suffice.

Scorpios usually keep their feelings and thoughts to themselves, for they are too deep for mere words. However, they do not hesitate to make the perfect comment at the perfect time, especially if it will deflate someone's pompous ego. Scorpios must avoid their tendency to test their lovers against the most extreme of hypothetical circumstances. That can distract them from listening to advice that can help them become more powerful individuals.

What Scorpios Look For

Seriousness and wisdom are two traits that appeal to Scorpios. They like someone with sexual appeal, yet their taste is not likely to reflect the stereotypical image of good looks and sexiness. A quirky sense of humor and a unique perspective on life appeal to them. A Scorpio may often be attracted to someone whom they may feel they have known and loved in a previous lifetime.

If Scorpios Only Knew

If Scorpios only knew that they were not being judged as harshly as they sometimes judge others, they would relax more and not put so much stress on themselves to succeed in everything they do. Scorpios work very hard to impress other people with their efforts, but the one they want most to impress is themselves. This is complicated by the fact that they feel they are being graded, perhaps unable to achieve the high standards they, and others, expect. They should know that it is no sin to take a day off once in a while to rest and regroup.

Marriage

Scorpio is loyal to his partner and does anything for her. But the person who marries a typical Scorpio must realize that Scorpio expects to dominate the partnership. The Scorpio has to feel proud of his partner and her skills, and he goes to great ends to enable his partner to achieve her ambitions, too. Scorpio shrewdness is a vital asset in any partnership.

A Scorpio who accepts orders from a partner does so for a particular reason. For example, if money or future progress is the reward, Scorpio acquiesces. Scorpio waits for as long as it takes to achieve the results he wants. It is unlikely for Scorpio and his partner to have a marriage without extreme ups and downs, and intense highs and lows.

Scorpio's Opposite Sign

Taurus is Scorpio's complementary sign, and even though the two share the virtues of loyalty, determination, and passion, they are very different in other ways. Taurus has the temerity to bring Scorpio down to earth with her own commonsense approach to living, and although Taurus is attracted to Scorpio's mysterious charm, she isn't overwhelmed by it. Scorpio is able to bring out the spiritual potential in Taurus' earthy nature, while Taurus teaches Scorpio how to be patient and sociable.

Pairing Up

In general, if people display the characteristics typical of their sign, intimate relationships between a Scorpio and another individual can be described as follows:

Scorpio with Scorpio:	Harmonious; two souls bound together by passion and honor
Scorpio with Sagittarius:	Harmonious, with Sagittarius' sense of fun a positive factor
Scorpio with Capricorn:	Harmonious, if Scorpio knows how to light Capricorn's fire
Scorpio with Aquarius:	Difficult, but a brilliant match when it works
Scorpio with Pisces:	Harmonious; one of the most intense and passionate love matches
Scorpio with Aries:	Turbulent; an almost impossible meld unless love finds a way
Scorpio with Taurus:	Difficult, yet Taurus can bring Scorpio down to earth
Scorpio with Gemini:	Turbulent, because free-spirited Gemini won't be controlled
Scorpio with Cancer:	Harmonious; a romance of great intensity

Scorpio with Leo:	Difficult, but exciting as lovers
Scorpio with Virgo:	Harmonious, so long as Scorpio doesn't try to dominate Virgo
Scorpio with Libra:	Harmonious, thanks to Libra's amiability and poise

If Things Don't Work Out

Scorpio has been known to harbor anger, resentment, and even revenge fantasies when a relationship ends. It can be very hard for Scorpio to see her own part in a romantic or marital failure, and even harder for her to move past the bad feelings it creates. However, a spiritually evolved Scorpio comes to understand that she must forgive herself and her partner for whatever went wrong in the relationship if she wishes to move on to better things.

Scorpio at Work

Sometimes Scorpios may have to be a bit cold-blooded to make sure that they get what is coming to them. They can be ruthlessly competitive about promotions, raises, and projects at work. Scorpios should not openly confront anyone unless they are absolutely sure that they have the resources on all levels to handle what could be used against them. Power struggles could get quite intense.

Scorpios may want to be less confrontational and work their will beneath the surface and behind the scenes. Scorpios usually benefit from being as secretive and subtle as they can be, but they should not let these traits undermine their effectiveness.

Scorpios should not reveal all of their dreams to just anyone. Scorpios need to learn how to use other people's money and resources to their advantage. If Scorpios have been working hard to obtain the trust of those they work with, they should ask for more responsibility, including handling other people's money. If that happens, Scorpios must treat it as a sacred trust.

Typical Occupations

Scorpios are well suited for work in banking, asset management, recycling, estate planning, detective work, the mantic arts (astrology, the tarot, and other occult subjects), magic, and matters related to sex. Police work, espionage, the law, physics, and psychology are all attractive professions for Scorpio.

Any occupation in which Scorpios feel important and that offers the opportunity to investigate and analyze complex problems will satisfy them. Their inner intensity and outer focus can result in the concentration of a surgeon, pathologist, or scientist. Any profession in which research or dealing with the solving of mysteries is present appeals to Scorpios. Their secretive natures make them natural detectives. They are also likely to succeed in any profession where detailed research is required.

They may be pharmacists, undertakers, insurers, market analysts, or members of the armed services. They can also excel as writers, journalists, and orators. They succeed because they know how to communicate the power of their convictions. Always drawn to extremes, Scorpios do very well working by themselves, or with many people in a large organization.

Behavior and Abilities at Work

In the workplace, a typical Scorpio:

* is relentless about completing a task
* appears to be confident in all situations
* may not work well as part of a group
* knows the importance of projects
* senses the moods and problems around him
* excels as a team leader
* is willing to put in extra effort on tough tasks
* is loyal and productive

Scorpio As Employer

A typical Scorpio boss:

- demands total loyalty
- helps people he likes
- knows how to get to the heart of the matter
- is secretive about his motives
- confronts a crisis directly
- is concerned if a crisis arises
- makes employees feel like part of a team
- can be ruthless

Scorpio As Employee

A typical Scorpio employee:

- is tenacious, yet calm
- does not waste time
- focuses on what she wants to achieve
- goes after what she wants
- won't accept failure till all attempts to succeed are exhausted
- is intense and career minded
- contributes extra time and effort
- is loyal and efficient
- works overtime when needed

Scorpio As Coworker

The person who works with a Scorpio can expect a passionate drive and unwavering loyalty, along with competitiveness and a dedication to success. The desks and offices of Scorpios are usually clean and neat, with equipment that helps them do their jobs better: reference books, software, and motivational CDs. They are shrewd analysts. Scorpios can work very hard, and they often provide an air of quiet confidence in a business.

Details, Details

People born during the time of Scorpio function best in their day-to-day responsibilities when they use their keen intuition as an aid to handling details. They can get to the heart of the matter without regard for diplomacy. Solving mysteries is their talent, and they can get to the root of any problem, human or mechanical. Scorpios enjoy putting together the "clues" they discover from listening to others to solve mysteries about people's motives and actions at work.

Scorpios are very hard workers and are unlikely to see any part of a task as being beneath them or their capabilities. Because they are not very talkative or apt to become involved in social cliques, it should not be assumed that they don't have good teamwork skills. A Scorpio is never too ego-centric to feel as if her contribution to a project must be major in order to fulfill an important role.

The penetrating gaze of a Scorpio is unlikely to miss any detail. Whether she is dealing with figures, outlines, or notes, she peruses the material to see how all the facts fit together. A Scorpio does not forget and usually does not forgive.

Money

Scorpios are inclined to receive awards or enter contests where their ability to discover or even just plain guess secrets wins them a prize. Scorpios are drawn to make money on subjects that have a magical, mystical, or detective theme about them. They might also receive gifts from others in the form of grants, scholarships, and inheritances. Scorpios should plan their estate or set up a trust fund—nothing lasts forever, and it is important that Scorpios plan for the transfer of resources after they leave this world.

Scorpios should be of a single mind about their desire to make money. A negative attitude towards wealthy people could sabotage efforts to become successful. However, they should take great care that they do not attempt to use their money as a means of power, because this always becomes a negative issue for them.

At Home

Scorpios often find it hard to relax. Many Scorpios try to relax by continuing to work, because of the intense pressure they put on themselves to finish everything before leaving for that much-needed rest. Their best policy is to have an alternative interest or hobby that they can pursue with passion, thus giving them relaxation from their main work.

Behavior and Abilities at Home

Scorpio typically:

* expresses herself with color
* is concerned about house security
* is gentle with the sick
* is protective
* guards her privacy
* likes subtle, quiet lighting
* enjoys lounging in underwear or lingerie

Leisure Interests

Scorpios pursue even their leisure interests at an intensity and depth of feeling that other signs would expect to feel about politics, or religion. They don't know the meaning of "it doesn't matter if you win or lose; it's how you play the game." Scorpios enjoy doing things that other people might find too risky or emotionally draining.

The typical Scorpio enjoys the following pastimes:

* browsing through flea markets and thrift shops
* reading detective and mystery novels

* researching ancient civilizations
* studying psychology
* competitive sports
* any game that requires shrewd tactics

Scorpio Likes

* being home
* sex
* intimacy
* privacy
* mysteries
* secrets
* money
* powerful people

Scorpio Dislikes

* shallow relationships
* feeling exposed
* revealing too much
* people who know more than they do
* too many compliments
* having to trust a stranger
* mysteries they can't solve
* ambivalence
* demeaning jobs

The Secret Side of Scorpio

Scorpio is all about secrets. Inside a typical Scorpio is a person who is so guarded that the secrets of Scorpio usually remain secret. All Scorpios like to keep their true nature as hidden as possible. They feel vulnerable to questions about their thoughts and behavior, and for this reason they may choose to stay away from other people born under their Sun sign who are likely to penetrate their emotional armor. Scorpio exercises power through emotion, intellect, and instinct.

Pluto

Pluto is the planet of power and transformation. It symbolizes the part of people that wants to get and use power of every kind. It is the planet of extremes, and so it rules people's personal power to do good, but it also rules power struggles, gangsters, dictators, and the terrible things that happen when people try to make themselves powerful at the expense of others. Pluto is associated with the mysteries of life, magic, sex, and, the ultimate transformation, death. It is also associated with resurrection, whether it be renovating a home, getting cosmetic surgery, or bringing back into a person's life something he thought was long gone. It represents the unconscious mind, invisible yet powerful enough to produce compulsions and obsessions seemingly beyond an individual's control. Like Pluto, their purpose is to help people become aware of what needs to be eliminated from their lives and to help them do so.

Bringing Up a Young Scorpio

Scorpio children are usually active, quick to learn, and intelligent. They have a deep and relentless curiosity that demands to be satisfied. They should be gently guided away from too much interest in forbidden areas, as they have a tendency to be fascinated by everything that is hidden and mysterious. Understanding the rights and needs of others is an important lesson for young Scorpios. In this way Scorpio children learn to forgive the hurts and mishaps of everyday life.

The best way to show love to a Scorpio child is to always be loyal and to make it possible for her to follow an interest in science, medicine, engineering, sports, or literature. Scorpio children who are not kept busy can become sullen, brooding over imagined slights from siblings or other children at school. At times a Scorpio child may feel like an outsider, so it is up to her parents to make her realize that everyone feels that way at times and it is simply a part of life.

A private space is essential for all Scorpio children—someplace where they can be alone and undisturbed. It could be a room of their own or just a closet. A secret hiding place gives the Scorpio child a sense of security.

The Scorpio Child

The typical Scorpio child:

* is very possessive of toys and belongings
* may have an imaginary playmate
* holds her fears inside
* is cautious with strangers
* is a good little detective
* enjoys a contest and likes to win
* learns from mistakes
* can be a discipline problem
* is loyal to family and friends
* gets revenge if crossed
* gets along well with adults

Scorpio As a Parent

The typical Scorpio parent:

* demands obedience
* is strict and stubborn

* is serious about rules
* keeps children active and involved
* enjoys participating in her child's interests
* can be overprotective
* cares passionately about the family
* finds it hard to admit to a mistake

Health

Scorpios are quite often physically strong and enjoy good health. However, some Scorpio individuals do have a tendency to put on weight in later life. Known as the sexiest sign, Scorpios need to release their stress and tension with lovemaking. Their emotions run very deep and their physical needs are great. Nose and throat problems, bladder disorders, and problems with the reproductive organs are the most common Scorpio illnesses. People born under this sign benefit from taking antioxidants. Scorpios have amazing recuperative powers, and though they are rarely ill, they are likely to recover speedily when they are.

FAMOUS SCORPIOS

Marie Antoinette

Richard Burton

Prince Charles

Hillary Rodham Clinton

Christopher Columbus

Leonardo DiCaprio

Sally Field

Jodie Foster

Bill Gates

Whoopi Goldberg

Goldie Hawn

Grace Kelly

Robert F. Kennedy

Vivien Leigh

Joni Mitchell

Demi Moore

Mike Nichols

Joaquin Phoenix

Pablo Picasso

Julia Roberts

Theodore Roosevelt

Meg Ryan

Carl Sagan

Sam Shepard

Ted Turner

"The starry vault of heaven is in truth the open book of cosmic projection."

—CARL GUSTAV JUNG

SAGITTARIUS
November 22–December 21

SAGITTARIUS
November 22–December 21

Planet: Jupiter

Element: Fire

Quality: Mutable

Day: Thursday

Season: autumn

Colors: purple (all shades)

Plants: hydrangea, saffron, rosemary

Perfume: peony

Gemstones: amethyst, turquoise, garnet, tanzanite

Metal: pewter

Personal qualities: Generous, cosmopolitan, humorous, optimistic, well traveled, and honest to a fault

Keywords

We call the following words "keywords" because they can help you unlock the core meaning of the astrological sign of Sagittarius. Each keyword represents issues and ideas that are of supreme importance and prominence in the lives of people born with Sagittarius as their Sun sign. You will usually find that every Sagittarius embodies at least one of these keywords in the way she makes a living:

freedom • professorial • teaching • learning • spirituality
world traveler • philosophy • expansion • enlarge • increase
integrate • encourage • prosper • jovial • positive outlook • luck

wealth • generosity • bounty • broad perspective
higher education • law • philosophy • religion
broadcast journalism • publishing world • exotic cuisine
tolerance • souvenirs • idealistic friendship
worldview • gambling

Sagittarius' Symbolic Meaning

The symbol for Sagittarius is Chiron, the bow-wielding Centaur—half man and half horse. Chiron the Centaur was the first doctor of herbal medicine and a wise sage. In Greek mythology, he was the teacher of the great warrior Achilles. Chiron's archetype is the Wounded Healer, who, through his own pain and experience, learns to heal others.

The legend of Chiron may have begun with stories of a wise and skillful hunter, perhaps the leader of the first tribe to hunt from horseback. The other tribes might have seen them as being half man and half horse. Travel on horseback made it possible for people to see many different places and tribes with unique customs. When they returned, they kept their own tribe hypnotized with stories of these far-off lands and peoples.

Those born under the sign of Sagittarius share this love of travel, animals—especially horses—the great outdoors, natural healing, and all things foreign. They are the philosopher-teachers of the zodiac, and without this vital function each generation would be forced to start from scratch without the accumulated wisdom of the ages to guide them. Not only do Sagittarians keep the torch of learning alight; they actively seek out knowledge and the wisdom to use it properly. They are interested only in the ultimate truth because, otherwise, it would not be worth knowing and teaching to others. The aim of every Sagittarian is to learn as much as she can about as many subjects as possible.

Sagittarians have a reputation for being blunt. Sagittarians feel that anyone who is telling the truth should be able to defend her position against any question. Sagittarians are in a hurry and want to keep traveling, learning, and sharing what they've learned.

Sagittarius is one of the four Mutable Sun signs in astrology (the other three are Gemini, Virgo, and Pisces). Mutable signs are associated with change, motion, and restlessness. People born under Mutable Sun signs understand flow and the need for constant readjustment.

Sagittarius is also one of three Fire signs (Aries and Leo are the other two). Fire signs are impulsive, energetic, quick to anger, and quick to forgive.

Sagittarians are not uncomfortable exposing even the most private areas of their lives to public scrutiny. Although they are often learned and sophisticated by nature, their natural honesty adds a delightful element of naïveté to their personality. Never expect them to apologize for having annoyed someone when they were only trying to get at the truth.

Recognizing a Sagittarius

People who exhibit the physical characteristics distinctive of the sign of Sagittarius look strong and active. Their eyes are steady, intelligent, bright, open, and honest. They are often taller than average, appear self-confident, and retain a youthful look.

A Sagittarian's face often appears about to break into a smile. Sagittarians use their hands and arms to make broad, sweeping gestures.

Sagittarius' Typical Behavior and Personality Traits

* pursues learning, teaching, and study
* says exactly what is on her mind
* enjoys taking risks
* is witty and can tell funny jokes
* has a good memory for facts
* needs freedom in relationships
* can laugh about her misfortunes

- is kindhearted, though tactless
- often has unconventional attitudes
- has to tell the truth
- can be cuttingly sarcastic
- strikes out when hurt

What Makes a Sagittarius Tick?

The lesson for Sagittarians to learn is that there is an important reason their life does not provide them with as many opportunities to travel, learn, and teach as they would like. They have come into the world with the astrological sign Sagittarius because they want to learn how to study, travel, and especially teach. They can expand their understanding of the way the world works through travel, certainly, but also through travel in their mind via philosophy and learning.

The Sagittarius Personality Expressed Positively

Sagittarians are naturally playful and good-humored. They have a laid-back, philosophical view about life and people that keeps them from taking themselves, their problems, and their concerns too seriously. At their very best they are self-deprecating and free-spirited. Although they are likely to have some firm opinions on many issues, they are the spirit of tolerance.

On a Positive Note

Sagittarians displaying the positive characteristics associated with their sign also tend to be:

- inspiring and stimulating
- optimistic and enthusiastic
- interested in diversity
- honest and fair-minded
- spiritual

- frank and open
- adventurous
- forgiving, without holding grudges
- generous

The Sagittarius Personality Expressed Negatively

When Sagittarians channel the negative side of their nature, they may appear to be rather priggish and self-righteous. If they are extremely religious they can have problems getting along with people who don't share their moral view. Also, because they are never hesitant to share their opinions with others, they can find it difficult to keep from lecturing people, hoping to convert them to their point of view.

Negative Traits

Sagittarians displaying the negative characteristics associated with their sign also tend to be:

- feisty and impatient
- blundering and careless
- preachy
- afraid of any heavy responsibility
- gamblers at heart
- indulgent of their own cravings
- roamers, never settling down
- failures at planning adequately
- potentially fanatical

Ask a Sagittarius If...

Ask a Sagittarius if you need a worldly perspective on a spiritual matter, since many Sagittarians have the sort of wisdom that is able to cross the boundaries of both points of view. You can also depend on people born under the influence of this sign to spin a good "yarn." Not only do they seem to have read just about everything, but their own life experiences are about as interesting as it gets. They're never too shy to talk about them, either.

Sagittarians As Friends

Sagittarians respond to all calls for help. They take in stray animals and stray people and support any cause in the name of friendship. They lend friends money without expecting to be repaid. Sagittarians have friends from many walks of life. Among them are likely to be a mixture of ethnic groups, both men and women, a range of ages, and straight and gay people; they are all treated as equals.

Sagittarians accept any friend who lives up to their personal standards. They defend their friends with great loyalty, but they also say exactly what they think. Close friendship with just one or two people is not the Sagittarian norm. In fact, anyone who tries to get too familiar with or who takes advantage of the Sagittarian natural friendliness may be struck by Sagittarians' brutal honesty, which can sometimes cut like a dagger.

Looking for Love

If a Sagittarian does not have a relationship, taking or planning a trip may very well bring one. Learning a language and going to the library or other places to learn would also expose a Sagittarius to new ideas and people. She might even find herself involved with someone who is foreign or different in some way, or whose family is from a different part of the world. A Sagittarius might be involved in broadcasting, publishing, travel, philosophy, or research, and those interests will lead her to meet a mate.

More often than not, Sagittarians do not consciously look for a partner. Instead, they purposefully put themselves in a variety of social circumstances where they have the opportunity to meet a great many interesting people. Many times a Sagittarian romance begins with friendship, which may be one of the reasons the people born under this sign have so many friends! Or, because they always seem to be surrounded by friends, it is natural that at times a Sagittarian is set up on a date by those same well-meaning friends. Occasionally this works out favorably, but sometimes it can backfire. Ultimately, Sagittarius is the best judge of whom he will find interesting.

A Sagittarius cannot live his life based on the opinions or the gossip of others. Keeping this in mind will bring awareness of influences for finding a mate that may be coming from newspapers, magazines, books, TV, radio, or other outside sources, and not just through people a Sagittarius actually knows.

Finding That Special Someone

Casual conversation has the potential to lead to true love for Sagittarians, since it is by sharing experiences and ideas that they are most likely to find their special someone. If Sagittarius is looking to find a partner, going on a singles cruise or even just taking a trip can lead her to her soul mate.

First Dates

Sagittarians don't really like "dates" in the traditional sense. They prefer spontaneous meetings. An afternoon coffee date can turn into a conversation that lasts till midnight. A Sagittarian can find love in the great outdoors. Taking part in or even watching sporting events is a favorable way for Sagittarius to find, maintain, and improve a relationship. A nature excursion or picnic would be great for a first date. Just going out for a walk together—especially to a library or bookstore—would make a Sagittarius happy.

Sagittarius in Love

Sagittarians enjoy the physical pleasures of love. They are inventive, very generous, and good-natured when they are in a relationship. Although

---

affectionate and loving, Sagittarians are totally honest with their loved ones. Sagittarians are not apt to be too demonstrative: not much cuddling, showering of gifts, or gifts of flowers—a character trait that may be misconstrued as lack of warmth and consideration. However, they will make it exciting for their beloved in other ways—deep philosophical discussions and good intellectual compatibility.

Undying Love

Sagittarians see romance as an adventure, intellectually, physically, and emotionally. Any fears they harbor about falling deeply in love are because they feel they will give away a piece of their soul, or need to change more about their life than is comfortable for them. They rarely second-guess their choices in love, but because they are a Fire sign, the sparks may die down and Sagittarius may want to go back to being "just friends" again. They may feel wistful, but more likely they sense that this is a favorable experience that has simply come to an end.

Expectations in Love

Someone who shares her ideals, a sense of fun, love of ideas, and zest for life would be the right companion to make a Sagittarius feel secure in love. She expects her loved one to be open-minded, to stimulate, to amuse, and to give her freedom of movement, not tie her down. Sagittarius won't be attracted to someone who is not able to keep up with her pace and her desire to travel and explore.

Sagittarians are loving and playful people and actually make good parents. But, as risk takers and adventurers, they are often attracted to danger in their love affairs. They want a partner who enjoys spontaneity and who appreciates their honesty, courageous outbursts, and enthusiasm. They also want a partner who does not try to control them. Although passion is an important part of a romantic relationship, they also need to feel as if they are best friends with a lover. For them, friendship is the gateway to true personal intimacy and love.

What Sagittarians Look For

Sagittarians are not looking for a person to validate their attitudes or their views. But they are happiest when they can be with someone who is as intellectually curious as they tend to be. It is the intensity of someone's dedication to their own ideas and not the ideas themselves that excites Sagittarians. For example, it is not unusual for a Sagittarian to fall in love with a person whose political, religious, or philosophical ideas are quite different from their own views. This makes for lively debate, another Sagittarian fondness.

If Sagittarians Only Knew...

If Sagittarians only knew that they could find much of the happiness they are looking for in their proverbial backyard, they might not feel as if they had to go so far afield to find it. While they congratulate themselves on being able to see things from a wide perspective, they should know that it is the details of day-to-day life that actually make up most of the bigger issues.

Marriage

The person who contemplates becoming the marriage partner of a typical Sagittarius must realize that Sagittarius values his freedom above everything. In return, the person who partners Sagittarius can expect honesty and plenty of creative ideas.

Frank and friendly, Sagittarius wants a partner who can love him for his outspoken charm, not get hurt by it. His words and actions always show what he is thinking and feeling, so a potential partner should be quite clear about articulating her opinions and feelings, as well. Sagittarians don't play games when it comes to love; they want a partner who is not weak and who does not retreat. In marriage, a partner must always ask—never tell—the Sagittarius to do something. Sagittarians do not respond well to authority.

Sagittarius' Opposite Sign

Quick-witted, mercurial Gemini is Sagittarius' complementary sign, and although there are some definite similarities between the two signs—intellectual curiosity and a love of conversation—there are also many things they can learn from each other. Gemini has an eye for details that helps broad-minded Sagittarius fill in the blanks. Plus, Gemini gives great parties and has a special talent for treating every conversation as if it is the best she's ever heard. Sagittarius' "no harm, no foul" attitude toward life teaches Gemini to be less anxious.

Pairing Up

In general, if people display the characteristics typical of their sign, intimate relationships between a Sagittarius and another individual can be described as follows:

Sagittarius with Sagittarius:	Harmonious; lifetime lovers and best friends
Sagittarius with Capricorn:	Harmonious, if Capricorn can learn to be more carefree
Sagittarius with Aquarius:	Harmonious; these two are made for each other in every way
Sagittarius with Pisces:	Difficult, unless Pisces can be less needy
Sagittarius with Aries:	Harmonious; a passionate partnership
Sagittarius with Taurus:	Turbulent, if Taurus attempts to control Sagittarius
Sagittarius with Gemini:	Difficult, but the partners have the ability to challenge each other
Sagittarius with Cancer:	Turbulent, because Cancer is security conscious

Sagittarius with Leo:	Harmonious, though Leo can be stubborn
Sagittarius with Virgo:	Difficult, since they are emotional opposites
Sagittarius with Libra:	Harmonious, with a shared enthusiasm for life and love
Sagittarius with Scorpio:	Harmonious, unless Scorpio makes too many demands

If Things Don't Work Out

Sagittarians need freedom and do not do well with a possessive, clingy, or emotionally demanding partner. Sagittarians are usually quite generous, and so dislike pettiness in others. These differences, more than any other, are likely to be the reasons for a breakup. Sagittarians don't often suffer through a dramatic parting; despite their winsome ways, they are really quite practical people. Even when they have decided to separate from a lover or marriage partner, they generally manage to remain friends.

Sagittarius at Work

When Sagittarians are required to act immediately, without having the time to think about what they are doing, they possess the courage to do anything they need to do. However, when they are allowed the luxury of enough time to think about what is required of them, they are inclined to be timid and cautious. It is important that Sagittarians not become so inspired by each new piece of wisdom they learn that they decide to put off the plans of yesterday to make yet another grand plan to change their life, and then cancel their plans tomorrow when new information becomes available.

It is also important that Sagittarians avoid their tendency to resist taking care of the details necessary to implement any successful plan. No sign is as fearless and broad-minded as Sagittarius is when it comes to encountering the new and the strange, yet Sagittarians need to develop tolerance for the necessary and the routine. By improving their education and job skills, especially management skills, they learn how best to delegate. Expending extra effort on studies comes back to a dedicated Sagittarius tenfold.

Typical Occupations

Professions that are good for a Sagittarius include travel, higher education, broadcasting, publishing, research, politics, motion pictures—especially documentaries—and writing books, as opposed to writing articles. Whatever Sagittarians do, they should approach it as a lifelong learning experience, rather than a job. They respond to the grand sweep of ideas and must have a career that allows them to share those ideas with others.

Sagittarians are versatile people. They are by nature teachers and philosophers. Nothing is better play to a Sagittarian than expounding on the moral principles, laws, and ideas that explain the universe. Through these traits they serve well as theologians or scientists.

They are also suited to the law, public service, or social administration. They do well in public relations, advertising, publishing, broadcasting, the Internet, as well as anything to do with the travel industry. Many Sagittarians are found in jobs that allow them to exercise their natural desire to see the world. Working outdoors, in sports or fitness, and with horses or other animals are ideal choices.

Behavior and Abilities at Work

In the workplace, the typical Sagittarius:

* is versatile and multitalented
* gets tired when bored
* needs to do several things at once
* may have to get outside
* has creative ideas
* needs physical and intellectual exercise

Sagittarius As Employer

A typical Sagittarius boss:

- is generally optimistic
- can market and sell anything well
- may be quite blunt and expects people to say what they mean
- thinks outside the box
- may be hard to pin down
- fights for what she believes is right
- is broad-minded and thinks of the bigger picture
- may overlook details

Sagittarius As Employee

A typical Sagittarius employee:

- works best when allowed freedom
- is cheerful and good-natured
- lifts everyone's spirits with humor
- responds quickly if his help is needed
- needs to be appreciated
- is usually a fast worker
- is enthusiastic and interested
- learns and expands his knowledge

Sagittarius As Coworker

Sagittarians do well working with others, as they tend to be very generous and tolerant. In this way, they gain their coworkers' trust and confidence. A Sagittarian's expanded awareness enables her to deal with any petty jealousies that may arise with her successes. A Sagittarius should have sympathy for and from those she might have envied at one time, but she should also extend her compassion to those who are not as fortunate.

Details, Details

Many Sagittarians think of details as boring necessities. If they can delegate these details, they do so, so that they themselves can concentrate on broader concepts and the creative end of projects. Sagittarians don't think small. They believe that it is best to think big, as if one owned the company one works for. It is important for them to break out of boring routines.

Sagittarians are better with details than they think. They remember names, birthdays, and other bits of information regarding the people they work with. They have a tremendous grasp of figures and can translate their meaning to more personal concepts. When they are told that they are good at these things, though, they may doubt the compliment.

Still, when they must deal with details on a regular basis, they have the potential to learn something vital. The process can teach them about time-tables and how to stick to a schedule. Once Sagittarians understand that being good with detail-oriented matters does not interfere with their talent for big ideas, they are sure to become more amenable to working within smaller facets of a project.

Money

Wealth and success may come to a Sagittarius through sports, everything that is natural and pure, animals—especially horses—philosophy, travel, justice, broadcasting, and publishing.

Handling money is a Sagittarian weakness. Economy does not come naturally to generous, expansive Sagittarians, so a few practical lessons should be taken into consideration; for example, rash spending should be curtailed. These restless, freedom-loving personalities need to learn that there are some financial planning rules that should be learned for their own good. Another weakness can be their certainty that they can gain a windfall through gambling or some other game of chance.

At Home

Sagittarians make their home wherever they happen to be; some have, or would like, several homes, while others may be permanent travelers. It is not unusual for Sagittarians to spend time living abroad, or to divide their time between two different countries.

Behavior and Abilities at Home

Sagittarius typically:

- is planning for the next trip
- likes to be casual and laid-back
- has mementos of travels around the house
- enjoys making and receiving social visits
- loves informal decor
- is not a "neat freak"
- loves to entertain friends and associates

Leisure Interests

Sagittarian leisure interests are varied and versatile. Sports are natural activities for Sagittarians, who enjoy the social contact as much as the competition. Long-distance travel to foreign places is one of the main Sagittarian interests. Some may prefer to "travel" in the world of literature, religion, or philosophy.

The typical Sagittarius enjoys the following pastimes:

- reading about other cultures
- risky sports or gambling
- breeding animals and keeping pets
- travel and exploration abroad
- taking courses in philosophy
- studying foreign languages
- gatherings related to religion and spirituality

Sagittarius Likes

* freedom and being on the move
* alternative ideas
* luggage
* natural remedies
* inviting friends over for dinner
* lotteries and raffles
* new books
* parties and flirting
* workout clothes
* exotic dishes

Sagittarius Dislikes

* being sedentary
* disapproval from others
* making commitments
* being too confined
* doing the dishes
* taking care of details
* having to get dressed up
* small talk
* close mindedness
* formality
* having to be on time

The Secret Side of Sagittarius

Inside anyone who has strong Sagittarian influences is a person who wants to be free. Possessive partners, conservative thinkers, and bureaucrats with whom Sagittarius comes into contact should be aware of this. The

Sagittarian who is held back in life, in love, or in opportunity for spiritual growth will be unhappy.

Like the Centaur, one of the Sagittarian symbols, Sagittarius exercises conflict between mind and body. His purpose is to overcome this conflict so he may guide others.

Jupiter

Jupiter, the biggest planet in our solar system, rules expansion, growth, the big picture, thinking big, being jovial, and being fortunate. Jupiter rules plain luck, but also the fortune that is the result of expanding one's mind through learning and being open to new ideas. It rules expansion of all kinds, whether buying another business, adding a room, or increasing the size of our waistlines. When Jupiter energies are operating in your life, things will not go badly even if you do nothing at all.

Influenced by Jupiter, a person may go overboard in his enjoyment of the finer things in life and become a real "high liver." It's no wonder that Jupiter is said to rule the liver as well as the blood, veins, and arteries, as they carry life to the farthest reaches of our bodies, and our hips and thighs, which help to move us around the Earth.

Bringing Up a Young Sagittarius

Most young Sagittarians enjoy learning but dislike being held back by what they see as needless rules. They are capable of setting their own standards and should be encouraged to do so. Sagittarian children hide their hurts, disappointments, and sorrows behind an optimistic belief that everything is bound to get better. The clown who laughs while her heart is breaking is behaving in a very Sagittarian way. It is important that the Sagittarian child be allowed to take advantage of opportunities for learning and socializing. It would also be an excellent idea to ensure that she has a higher education waiting for her when she is ready.

Sagittarian children may often question adult values and are eager to point out any adult hypocrisy that they notice. The best thing that the parents of a Sagittarian child can do is to be totally honest. In the case of young Sagittarius, there should be no pressure or possessiveness, but love should be given by way of encouragement and by showing pleasure. Broaden young Sagittarians' horizons in every way possible. Giving them the means to travel is a good way, though traveling with them is best.

The Sagittarius Child

The typical Sagittarius child:

- is impulsive and adventurous
- is happy and playful
- is active and gets bumps and bruises as a result
- is interested in many subjects
- expects total honesty
- enjoys being with others
- loves to play outdoors
- asks endless questions
- adores pets and animals
- rarely sits still
- enjoys being read to

Sagittarius As a Parent

The typical Sagittarius parent:

- thinks globally, not locally
- always answers questions honestly
- has faith in children
- provides access to a good education
- is eager to talk and play with children

- ✳ is stimulating company and fun, too
- ✳ encourages children to travel when older
- ✳ may expect too much intellectually
- ✳ exposes children to diversity

Health

Adventurous and active, Sagittarians fear being ill or confined. As they are so full of life, their energy levels fluctuate and often get depleted. They should watch out for excess weight around the hip and thigh areas, which are the parts of the body that Sagittarius rules.

Typical Sagittarians are healthy and energetic. Any kind of routine taxes the Sagittarian optimism. However, their positive outlook helps them to overcome illnesses quickly.

Sagittarians tend to take physical risks, so accidents arising from dangerous sports can be expected from time to time. The jovial Jupiter influence can lead a Sagittarian into indulgence in food or drink, which may lead to health problems.

FAMOUS SAGITTARIANS

Woody Allen

Kim Basinger

Ludwig van Beethoven

William Blake

Noel Coward

Winston Churchill

George Armstrong Custer

Sammy Davis, Jr.

Emily Dickinson

Joe DiMaggio

Walt Disney

Jane Fonda

Christopher Fry

Uri Geller

Jimi Hendrix

Bruce Lee

Bette Midler

Julianne Moore

Jim Morrison

Brad Pitt

Frank Sinatra

Steven Spielberg

Ben Stiller

Tina Turner

Mark Twain

"Anyone can be a millionaire, but to become a billionaire you need an astrologer."

—J. P. MORGAN

CAPRICORN
December 22–January 19

CAPRICORN
December 22–January 19

Planet: Saturn

Quality: Cardinal

Element: Earth

Day: Saturday

Season: winter

Colors: black, dark brown, gray

Plants: pansy, ivy, tulip, lilac

Perfume: vetiver

Gemstones: jet, obsidian, smoky quartz, turquoise

Metal: lead

Personal qualities: Ambitious, prudent, self-disciplined, thrifty, and traditional

Keywords

We call the following words "keywords" because they can help you unlock the core meaning of the astrological sign of Capricorn. Each keyword represents issues and ideas that are of supreme importance and prominence in the lives of people born with Capricorn as their Sun sign. You will usually find that every Capricorn embodies at least one of these keywords in the way she makes a living:

status quo • seriousness and maturity • materialism
organization • responsibility • structure • crystallization

permanence • tradition • conservatism • fears
caution • leader of the pack • realism
definition and understanding of rules and limits
test of time • authority figures • discipline • concern
fulfill obligations • test • concentration • endure restriction
scaling the mountain • leadership potential • timeline • wisdom

Capricorn's Symbolic Meaning

A mountain goat symbolizes Capricorn. The mountain goat is tireless as it makes its way to the tops of mountain after mountain. Most Capricorns are equally tireless in their efforts to get to the top of their respective professions. Most people might think that Capricorns desire above all to attain the respect of the masses. It is more accurate to say that they crave the respect of those whom they, themselves, respect. This is as important to them as is living in wealth and style, yet another way they gain the respect of the "in crowd."

To get to the top, Capricorns are willing to do what is expected of them. This gets them the reputation of being conservative, when deep inside, they are quite sensual. They are conservative in the best sense of the word. Capricorns conserve what they have so that they will have enough when they need it. This is true practicality. Capricorns make wonderful executives. In fact, it is difficult for them to show their true worth until they are left alone to assume some kind of definite responsibility. When they feel this weight resting on their shoulders and realize that the success of the endeavor is up to them, they rise to the occasion, succeeding where others would give up. Once they make something of themselves, they display a kind of energy that can overcome almost any obstacle.

Capricorns display this personality trait because Capricorn is one of the four Cardinal Sun signs in astrology (the other three are Aries, Libra, and Cancer). Cardinal signs approach life with a great deal of drive. They are enterprising, love to be on the go, and initiate new activities. They accomplish their goals. Capricorn is also one of the three Earth Sun signs in astrology (the other two are Taurus and Virgo). Earth signs respond to the world through their five senses: what they see, hear, taste, touch, and smell. This Earth-element energy gives Capricorns patience, discipline, and a great understanding of how the world works.

Their awareness of how far they have to go to achieve the respect they crave can sometimes make Capricorns pessimistic or, less often, depressed. This tendency actually comes not from the realization of how far they have to go, but from the fact that they rarely allow themselves to become inspired and energized by what they have already accomplished.

Recognizing a Capricorn

A typical Capricorn has a serious look, an "earthy" attractiveness. Capricorns generally do not smile a lot. A Capricorn is quite conscious of appearances, and cares about what other people think. Young Capricorns often look older than their years, and it is also typical for aging Capricorns eventually to become more relaxed and so look younger than their years. They walk with determination and discipline.

Capricorn's Typical Behavior and Personality Traits

* dresses according to convention
* is close to family, even distant relatives
* is somewhat self-conscious
* is quite moody and melancholy
* needs to gain recognition for work
* runs a well-organized home and office
* seems unapproachable
* is dignified and very polite
* appears self-protective

* is cautious when getting to know people
* likes to set long-term goals
* is very reliable
* has strong opinions
* seems as steady as a rock

What Makes a Capricorn Tick?

The lesson for Capricorns centers on the important reason that their life does not provide them with as many opportunities to enjoy success, wealth, and happiness as they would like. They have come into this world with the astrological sign Capricorn because they want to learn the best way to achieve success, wealth, and happiness! They know in their hearts that there are actual techniques they need to learn and lessons they need to apply in their lives before they can attain their full potential.

The Capricorn Personality Expressed Positively

Surefooted and thoroughly practical, in the end the Capricorn goat always reaches the heights, beating others who are faster but less determined. He knows that substance and endurance will win out over flash and style every time. A Capricorn who is true to himself may appear to be somewhat cold and emotionally detached, yet those born under this sign are also generous and kindhearted.

On a Positive Note

Capricorns displaying the positive characteristics associated with their sign also tend to be:

* good at organizing
* respectful of authority
* cautious, realistic, and conventional
* hardworking and scrupulous

- ambitious and good at business
- people with high standards
- individuals who honor traditions
- givers of sound advice
- calculating before taking action

The Capricorn Personality Expressed Negatively

A Capricorn who is frustrated or unhappy will have trouble getting along with people unless she is the one in authority. Capricorns are emotional but may choose to hide their feelings for fear of appearing weak. They can be a depressing influence on others, due to their rather stoic nature. Because success matters so much to them, they may be opportunistic at times.

Negative Traits

Capricorns displaying the negative characteristics associated with their sign tend to be:

- melancholy
- fatalistic
- rarely satisfied
- cynical and unforgiving
- selfish
- plodding
- manipulative
- egotistical
- loners

Ask a Capricorn If...

Ask a Capricorn if you want a practical solution to a problem. The people born under this sign pride themselves on their common sense. They may not have a glamorous approach to problems, but they know how to get the job done. You can always depend on Capricorns to make an honest and fair assessment. They manage to tell the truth without sounding critical.

Capricorns As Friends

Capricorns are loyal, kind, dependable, and often very generous to friends. They try to prove their sincerity by showing total devotion to the friendship. Capricorns like a friend who is patient, understanding, good mannered, and not too extroverted. They continue to love friends who are old or disabled. They do not desert or neglect loyal friends, no matter how bad the circumstances.

If a friendship fails because of bad judgment on their part, Capricorns can turn very negative. They will brood for days and weeks, mulling over an argument or a poor decision. Capricorns have an irritating habit of recommending things that they think will be good for a friend, but that the friend does not want. At their very worst, Capricorns may ruthlessly use a friend to further an ambition.

Looking for Love

A Capricorn may find that she is attracted to a person who reminds her of the parent she most respected or was disciplined by. This tendency could also manifest as an older person being her perfect partner. Capricorns often seem wise beyond their years, and for this reason they are likely to draw someone older into their sphere.

If a Capricorn does not have a love relationship, the reason is probably related to how she feels about structure, limits, and discipline. A Capricorn may be so disciplined that she does not leave any room in her life for a relationship, possibly because she thinks it will distract her from more serious, important matters. It could also be that a Capricorn does not want to get involved with anyone who displays either too much or too little self-discipline. She must be willing to share the stage with the person she loves and not be adamant about being the one in charge. A Capricorn must be careful not to be too limited in her thinking or unwilling to give people a chance to be human.

If a Capricorn is not in a committed relationship, then one is most likely to come during work hours or through interactions with authority figures. It could come at her place of employment, but not necessarily. Partners could tend to be older, and there might be an element of teacher and student in the relationship. Another way this might manifest is if a Capricorn met someone while she was functioning as an authority figure or working on becoming one.

Finding That Special Someone

Because of their devotion to work, Capricorns are likely to find their true love in the workplace or through a professional association of some sort. Since they have a busy social life, they have the chance to meet eligible singles at parties, at cultural events, or through the help of mutual friends. If they choose to use an online dating service, they are likely to keep it a secret from their friends because of their desire for privacy.

First Dates

Try the standard dinner and a movie for a first date for a Capricorn—an old movie, an Oscar winner, would be appropriate. A Capricorn is sure to appreciate it if the evening fits his idea of what a "good date" is. A concert is also a good choice. Capricorns appreciate good taste, so getting together for coffee and dessert at a posh bistro after an event is a good choice. It is always easier for Capricorns to relax and be themselves in an intimate social setting, and a visit to a jazz club or an elegant eatery conforms to their high standards.

Capricorn in Love

Typical Capricorns do not have casual affairs, and they say "I love you" only when they really mean it. They are realistic and down-to-earth and may worry about the emotional aspect of the relationship. Sometimes they must feel financially secure to enjoy love. It might be a good idea for a Capricorn to investigate working with her romantic partner in some practical way. When a Capricorn is in a relationship where she feels secure, then she is caring, considerate, and committed.

Undying Love

Even though Capricorns can fall in love quickly, they don't like to be the one to say the first "I love you." Fears of rejection may cause them to act the part of an aloof lover until the one they have set their eyes on speaks his or her intentions first. Despite this appearance of coyness, once they are part of a couple they are loyal to the point of being dogmatic. Romance often takes them by surprise, allowing them to show a sentimental side. Capricorn doesn't usually make great protestations of love, but will show his love in a hundred ways every day.

Expectations in Love

In their love relationships, Capricorns are very serious. They are usually slow to make approaches and almost never flirt just for fun. Capricorns are not inclined to have casual relationships. They desire to make a home and a family, to make a long-term commitment. Both Capricorn and his partner must state the level of commitment clearly before they make any move toward living together. Living together is the same thing as marriage for some, while for others it is an arrangement of convenience.

A Capricorn expects faithfulness and assumes she will be admired by her loved one. Love and relationships are also wrapped up with her work and career. If a partner is not doing well in those areas, there will be problems in the relationship, since the Capricorn partner may feel the need to criticize or be competitive. Capricorn may fear anyone who might try to impose any kind of discipline, limits, or structure. This would limit the number of people she could have a relationship with, but it is a part of the structure of a Capricorn's being and must be honored.

What Capricorns Look For

Capricorns are sensible people who are unlikely to fall for someone they consider flaky or unpredictable. Their traditionalist views are an important part of who they are, so they usually look for someone who is both serious and stable. They appreciate intelligence, as well as a person who is geared to becoming a success. A nonconformist or layabout is not likely to turn their head, even if good looks are a part of the package.

If Capricorns Only Knew...

If Capricorns only knew how respected and revered they are by the people around them, they would not worry about criticism and gossip affecting their reputation. Capricorns struggle to present themselves honestly, because they are afraid of how others will view them. One reason Capricorns are unwilling to let down their hair is their fear that they will appear to have the normal human frailties. So often they hold themselves to a higher standard, not realizing that it is the quest for perfection, not perfection itself, that makes them admirable.

Marriage

Capricorns seek a partner who has established a good, secure position in life. Rich or poor, if a Capricorn or his partner is not working or enjoying the same level of success or career satisfaction, the relationship will suffer. Capricorn wants a partner who can help him achieve his ambitions.

Capricorns tend to be workaholics, and it can be hard to get them home long enough to get relaxed and romantic. They tend to be strong, practical, and successful, however, and can provide their spouses with the best in life. Capricorns are very committed and serious about their lives, homes, and families.

The person who contemplates becoming the marriage partner of a typical Capricorn must realize that Capricorn will take over the organization of the partner's private and professional life. Given this, the person who partners Capricorn can expect responsibility, stability, and security.

Capricorn's Opposite Sign

Cancer is Capricorn's complementary sign, and even though these two are very different, it is possible for stoic Capricorn to learn a lot from Cancer's nurturing ways. Cancers can teach Capricorns how to relax and not take themselves so seriously. Because Cancers are in touch with their feelings, they can also make Capricorns understand that there is nothing wrong with being sensitive. Capricorn's work ethic inspires Cancer to strive harder to achieve goals.

Pairing Up

In general, if people display the characteristics typical of their sign, intimate relationships between a Capricorn and another individual can be described as follows:

Capricorn with Capricorn:	Harmonious, but is sometimes a marriage of convenience
Capricorn with Aquarius:	Harmonious, although may be somewhat lacking in passion
Capricorn with Pisces:	Harmonious, with Pisces nurturing Capricorn's ambitions
Capricorn with Aries:	Difficult, yet with plenty of romantic fireworks

Capricorn with Taurus:	Harmonious; a couple who seem to live in a world of their own
Capricorn with Gemini:	Turbulent, with lots of conflicting ideas and preferences
Capricorn with Cancer:	Difficult, yet these two have a lot to give each other
Capricorn with Leo:	Turbulent, but they make a glamorous pair
Capricorn with Virgo:	Harmonious; a true love match if there ever was one
Capricorn with Libra:	Difficult, but the challenge is well worth it
Capricorn with Scorpio:	Harmonious; an erotically charged relationship
Capricorn with Sagittarius:	Harmonious; lovers, friends, and partners in ambition

If Things Don't Work Out

If a relationship begins to fail, it often takes a Capricorn a long time to take action, as she has a strong sense of duty to her partner and her family. In general, Capricorns dislike divorce. Because of their intensely vulnerable nature, they fear the humiliation that comes with a breakup. Also, since the opinion of family members, friends, and even associates means a lot to them, they dislike having to explain a change in their marital or romantic status.

Capricorn at Work

A Capricorn wants to organize the company where she is employed, and she expects absolute loyalty and a disciplined routine. Her job may not be glamorous, but it provides her with a great opportunity to move ahead. Capricorns like coworkers to know that they are punctual and persistent and know how to structure their job and any business systems that they are responsible for in the most efficient and productive manner. By dressing and acting conservatively, Capricorns give a feeling of comfort to those above them.

If mistakes are being made by those in a position to help advance a Capricorn's career, then it is smart for the Capricorn to act cautiously. A Capricorn is calculating and does not want to do anything that might delay her reward or advancement. A Capricorn should do what she can to make things work smoothly, even if she has to fix things in such a way that no one realizes that she is making things work. Capricorn needs to be aware of her tendency to focus on her long-term career goals as much as or even more than on the job at hand. Her competence, professionalism, and perseverance will keep her from failing to do what must be done, but her long-term goals may often be best served by taking care of the day-to-day jobs, especially the ones that others are reluctant to do or unable to do well.

Typical Occupations

The occupations Capricorns usually choose are doctor, dentist, teacher, lawyer, banker, accountant, and any endeavor that deals with prestige or money. They naturally gravitate toward professions or jobs that support the status quo and where they can make a good living for themselves. Their quiet, ambitious natures are perfect for work under pressure. They also can succeed where projects demanding long-term planning are concerned. They generally make good architects, engineers, manufacturers, systems analysts, and researchers. Any occupation that requires good organization and smart management is appropriate for a Capricorn. Many Capricorns are art dealers, jewelers, and managers or agents for entertainers. They also have the ability to turn a failing business around.

Capricorns excel as bureaucrats or politicians due to their skill in debate. Capricorns prefer to work in private. Detail-oriented Capricorns make excellent managers. They are good with their hands, too, and may choose to be in construction or to work with farming, animals, and the land.

Behavior and Abilities at Work

In the workplace, a typical Capricorn:

* must have a comfortable and homey workspace
* is well organized
* is smart with money matters
* plans ahead and makes schedules
* works hard and for long hours
* likes to have food and drink available when working long hours

Capricorn As Employer

A typical Capricorn boss:

* takes responsibilities very seriously
* dresses conservatively and is well organized
* has a strong sense of duty and works very hard
* is kind but expects obedience to the rules
* likes family to visit him at work
* is a good administrator and director of operations
* may neglect personal needs for business

Capricorn As Employee

A typical Capricorn employee:

* stays with a company for a long time
* carries a heavy workload
* is conscientious and dependable
* expects a salary increase with time
* has respect for superiors
* enjoys commonsense assignments
* arrives very early and leaves late
* has an intelligent, wry sense of humor
* minds his own business

Capricorn As Coworker

Capricorns are something of an enigma as coworkers. Whether or not they are in a position of authority, they may instinctively take a leadership role. They are circumspect about their personal life and unlikely to talk to coworkers about life outside the workplace. Once Capricorns start on the road to success, their persistence and ability to focus on a goal enable them to succeed and become authority figures.

Details, Details

No matter how firmly Capricorns have fixed their gaze on the larger picture, they like having a say in the details, too. Capricorns often build their reputation on details, and should look for opportunities to show how worthy of promotion they are. They are sometimes being tested to see whether they should be able to join the club of those who are richer and more powerful than they are. It is important for a Capricorn to show how well she can delegate detail-oriented projects to others, since it can be hard for those born under the sign of the Goat to let other people have a hand in their work.

One of the problems Capricorns have in dealing with details is sometimes making them more important than the entire project. Getting bogged down in small matters can frustrate Capricorns to the point where they can't do their best work. They like having mastery over things, and handling detailed projects gives them this satisfaction. Capricorns need to learn that it is more important to show the full range of their abilities if they want to successfully establish themselves in a way that makes a difference.

Money

A Capricorn should always be conservative in the truest sense of the word, and should get involved in the conservation of resources of all kinds. This includes time, money, possessions, and both natural resources and those that are the result of manufacturing and technological processes.

While Capricorn rules prestige and the status quo, it is more common for people born under this sign to work to achieve a comfortable lifestyle than it is to have been born into money. Capricorns are materialistic people, though not necessarily in the negative sense of that word. They don't have to own fine things to appreciate them and know their worth. Capricorns are very good at positioning themselves in situations where they can accrue a lot of money, and once they have it, they know how to hold on to it.

At Home

Capricorns take great pride in maintaining a beautiful and well-appointed home. This is a representation not only of their success, but also of their need to create and preserve order in their environment. They are most comfortable in a home that is either like the one they grew up in or like the one they always wanted to have while growing up.

Behavior and Abilities at Home

Capricorn typically:

- likes having a routine
- really enjoys providing for the family
- takes pride in an organized household
- wants quality furniture and fixtures
- needs home as a showcase for business
- is devoted to home and family
- enjoys having visits from relatives
- is skilled as a decorator

Leisure Interests

Capricorns are so aware of their duties and responsibilities that they often find it very difficult to allow themselves to enjoy anything for its own sake. Most typical Capricorns are not much interested in team sports. They work hard at their hobbies and want to make a success of them. Whatever they choose to do, it must be respectable and increase their chances of being admired or honored.

The typical Capricorn enjoys the following pastimes:

* visiting museums and galleries
* golf, walking, playing chess
* gardening and improving the home
* reading best sellers
* music, either listening or playing
* attending exclusive parties

Capricorn Likes

* home and family
* duties and responsibilities
* history, antiques, and genealogy
* the "best" brands
* executive toys
* long naps and pure and simple food
* gemstones and jewelry
* membership at an exclusive club
* personalized gifts and monograms
* new books about old subjects

Capricorn Dislikes

* being pressured
* fads
* surprises
* disrespect

- being teased
- loneliness
- being unprepared
- being embarrassed
- forgetting her to-do list
- cheap quality
- criticism

The Secret Side of Capricorn

Capricorn people have very deep and real emotional needs that can slow them down considerably or even stop them in their tracks. Further contributing to their tendency toward depression are the pressures caused by their desire to maintain a prosperous appearance, keeping pace with both fashion and tradition, while at the same time living in luxury and ease and, in some way, above the level of those whose praises they seek.

Saturn

Saturn is the planet of structure, time, boundaries, restriction, and discipline. It helps people delay pleasure so that they can do what needs to be done in the time allotted. Saturn is a stern teacher, but it can reward individuals for enduring burdens in a mature manner. Conversely, if people shirk their responsibilities, Saturn will show them the error of their ways. Saturn is the last planet usually visible to the naked eye, and so it is associated with going as far as one can go in life, especially in one's career. It also rules automobiles, antiques, and crystals. Saturn is like an anchor, used to prevent people from drifting from where they should be. It rules the bones, teeth, and knees, as well as the sense of hearing.

Bringing Up a Young Capricorn

It is a good to teach Capricorn children the importance of respecting themselves and others for both their inner strength and their outer achievements. Usually, young Capricorns work doggedly at school subjects and aim to get good grades and gain honors. Little Capricorns need plenty of reassurance because they are natural worriers. It is good for them to learn that there is a time and place for everything. One of the unfortunate consequences of the instant TV/movie generation is that they see the story of successful people presented in a couple of hours or less. They have no idea how much dedication, work, rejection, disappointment, and self-motivation are necessary for a human being to build a successful life.

Young Capricorns are not particularly enthusiastic about sports or the outdoors, so they need to be encouraged to spend time outside in the fresh air getting some exercise. Trips to museums, visits to archeological sites, and even rock climbing are likely to satisfy them. They also need to be encouraged to relax and play. They may seem like very serious children, but they have a sense of humor, too. Young Capricorns can have trouble fitting in with other children their age, so they need to be brought into contact with young people who share their temperament.

The Capricorn Child

The typical Capricorn child:

* is well behaved and responsible
* likes to work on long-term projects
* enjoys setting goals
* can be highly competitive
* worries about her grades
* has respect for other people's things
* is serious but lightens up as he grows older

- usually formulates her life path early on
- has a good though often dark sense of humor
- plays at being an expert or authority figure
- seems older than his years
- likes to stay close to home
- enjoys school and contests of all kinds

Capricorn As a Parent

The typical Capricorn parent:

- teaches respect and responsibility
- takes parenthood seriously
- is caring and considerate
- will teach children about tradition
- is strict with rules but fair as well
- has a straight-faced sense of humor
- makes sure to provide a good education

Health

Capricorns need to learn to relax. Worry, long periods of work, and heavy responsibilities could lead to aches and pains and stress-related illnesses. Capricorns need to be careful of depression. They need to make sure to get enough rest at night, and enough light during the day. Capricorns usually exercise only if it fits into their work regime. Knees and bones are likely to be their vulnerable body parts. Their resistance to disease increases with age. Moderate in their habits, they often live to a ripe old age.

✧°✧  FAMOUS CAPRICORNS ✧°✧

Muhammad Ali

Isaac Asimov

Humphrey Bogart

Al Capone

Paul Cezanne

Mel Gibson

Barry Goldwater

Stephen Hawking

Howard Hughes

Joan of Arc

Janis Joplin

Diane Keaton

Martin Luther King, Jr.

Mary Tyler Moore

Kate Moss

Sir Isaac Newton

Richard Nixon

Dolly Parton

Edgar Allan Poe

Elvis Presley

Little Richard

Phil Spector

J.R.R. Tolkien

Denzel Washington

Tiger Woods

"Astrology is a language. If you understand this language, the sky speaks to you."

—DANE RUDHYAR

AQUARIUS
January 20–February 18

AQUARIUS
January 20–February 18

Planet: Uranus

Quality: Fixed

Element: Air

Day: Saturday

Season: winter

Colors: electric blue, sky blue, ultraviolet

Plants: tiger lily, bird of paradise, parsley

Perfume: lemon verbena

Gemstones: rock crystal, fluorite, azurite, lapis lazuli

Metal: uranium

Personal qualities: Unique, brilliant, inventive, articulate, and tolerant

Keywords

We call the following words "keywords" because they can help you unlock the core meaning of the astrological sign of Aquarius. Each keyword represents issues and ideas that are of supreme importance and prominence in the lives of people born with Aquarius as their Sun sign. You will usually find that every Aquarius embodies at least one of these keywords in the way he makes a living:

humanitarianism • inventive mind • detachment • idealism
radicalism • altruism • rebellion • progressivism
technical proficiency • eclecticism • genius • power to the people

futuristic • originality • chaos theory • free thinker • space travel
unusual • eccentricity • explosivity • excitability • surprise
electrify • rebel without a cause • upset • revolutionary • reform
liberated • UFO • the Internet

Aquarius' Symbolic Meaning

The symbol of the sign Aquarius is the Water Bearer pouring out his bounty to quench the thirst of world. For this reason, many people mistakenly think Aquarius is a Water sign. Water was the element the ancient sages connected with the realm of emotion, empathy, and intuition. However, Aquarius is not a Water sign. The element associated with Aquarius is Air, the realm of ideas. People born under Aquarius like to think in broad and theoretical terms and want to "pour out" their ideas to quench the intellectual thirst of the world. Being mistaken for a Water sign is a very significant clue to an important lesson for Aquarians. Water symbolizes emotions and empathy, and Aquarians are often perceived to be lacking in both.

Aquarians, concerned for the good of all, are inspired to invent solutions to society's problems. They are the mad scientists and absentminded professors of the zodiac. To do this requires a freethinking mind, unfettered by tradition or fear of disturbing the status quo. Aquarians learn from the past to change what they find distasteful in the present, for by doing that they create the future they envision. The emotional detachment necessary to see society's problems clearly and to try to solve them makes Aquarians seem to lack empathy for individuals' hardships. Aquarians should examine the actions they plan to take to make sure they will not be hurtful to others, even if hurting others is not their intent.

Aquarius is one of the four Fixed Sun signs in astrology (the other three are Taurus, Leo, and Scorpio). Fixed signs are concentrated, stubborn, and persistent. They are the ones who provide the stability to see things through. Aquarius is also one of the three Air signs in astrology (the other two are

Libra and Gemini). Air represents the mind, ideas, and the ability to think; Aquarian ideas may be unusual or even original, but once formed, they tend to remain fixed. Aquarians refuse to budge whenever an issue involves what they believe to be a matter of principle.

Once an Aquarian is finished thinking about a subject theoretically, she lets her scientific mind take a break and returns to the world of emotions. In fact, she can easily feel herself being overcome by feelings of empathy for those less fortunate. This is what inspires her in the first place to come up with solutions to society's urgent problems.

Recognizing an Aquarius

Aquarians often have a distant, dreamy look in their eyes. At other times their gaze is darting and anxious. They are likely to be taller than average, often with a lanky build that gives them a shambling walk. If their coloring is light, they are likely to be sandy haired. Aquarians may have an attractive, almost classic profile. Even if they are dressed expensively, their clothes never seem to fit quite right.

Aquarius' Typical Behavior and Personality Traits

* is friendly and easygoing
* likes groups and organizations
* can be totally eccentric
* is an intuitive thinker with a practical side
* has a wide variety of interests
* is involved with humanitarian causes
* has a mind of his own
* is detached at times
* has a very ethical, moral code
* is attracted to the mystical and the occult
* seeks to develop ideas and communicate them

* has a wide circle of friends from all walks of life
* accepts the many differences among people

What Makes an Aquarius Tick?

Aquarians are here to learn how to make real the future they can so easily see in their mind's eye! This is why their life does not provide them with as many opportunities as they would like to enjoy the freedom and other resources necessary to turn their innovative ideas into reality. In fact, they sometimes make such extreme changes that in their enthusiasm to get rid of the old ways they can destroy valuable things from the past that still have great usefulness.

The Aquarius Personality Expressed Positively

At their best, Aquarians are brilliant and engaging people who make friends with individuals from all walks of life. Despite being broad-minded, an ideal Aquarius has fixed ideas and stays true to them, even while being tolerant of other people's lifestyles, beliefs, and habits. Aquarius is often happiest when alone, so she can devote single-minded attention to her pet projects.

On a Positive Note

Aquarians displaying the positive characteristics associated with their sign also tend to be:

* inventive and original
* thoughtful and caring
* cooperative and dependable
* intensely interested in humanity
* strong supporters of political reforms
* independent thinkers
* loyal friends and advocates
* scientific and intelligent
* communicative

The Aquarius Personality Expressed Negatively

Frustrated or unhappy Aquarians may be rather crotchety, melancholy, and eccentric. They can be emotionally cold people and find it hard to show affection even for those closest to them. Despite their brilliant intelligence, negative Aquarians can be set in their ways and ideas. In extreme cases, they may even become hermits, unwilling to have their opinions assailed by other people.

Negative Traits

Aquarians displaying the negative characteristics associated with their sign also tend to be: .

* unwilling to compromise
* fanatical and unpredictable
* stubborn and tactless
* preoccupied with curiosities and weird obsessions
* perverse, with eccentric habits
* surprisingly lacking in confidence
* likely to shake up the status quo

Ask an Aquarian If...

Ask an Aquarian if you want a simple answer to a complex problem. It helps if your problem is not too emotionally based, but even if it is, an Aquarius will give it a try. The Aquarian mind is highly analytical and skilled at making quick assessments; turning a myriad of information into easy-to-follow directions is never difficult for the people of this sign. Also, if you don't get it the first time, an Aquarius never tires of explaining things, and never condescends.

Aquarians As Friends

An Aquarius friend is a constant source of mental stimulation, information, and practical help. Aquarians make many friends but few confidantes. Aquarius likes a friend who has intellectual interests and enjoys the unusual and the radical. She rarely passes judgment on the ethical codes of friends. Aquarius is friendly to anyone and tends to regard any relationship as platonic. An Aquarius takes great interest in her friends' ideas and projects, and enjoys giving advice and creative input. If an Aquarius wants to have the kind of friendships she has always dreamed of, she must avoid letting her tendency to go to extremes cause her to imagine that she must make radical changes that are really too much to ask of herself and others—changes that are bound to be too difficult to maintain.

Looking for Love

Getting involved with groups of people who have come together for a common goal will help an Aquarius find love. Aquarians can often find their soul mate through a circle of friends, or by getting involved with people who are in fraternal organizations, societies, clubs, trade unions, trade associations, environmental groups, political activist groups, chat rooms, theme cruises, tour groups, group therapy, and all other ways that people get together for mutual support. Going to a place established to help people meet potential partners is favored for this sign. Aquarians have a natural talent for turning their eyes on an individual and seeming to create the basis of a close relationship after only a few days, so long as there are shared opinions, ideas, and aims. An Aquarian may seek to combine love and activism, since she is likely to fall for an individual who is equally socially conscious and politically aware.

Going to completely different kinds of places to meet people—even places an Aquarian might previously have thought were too bizarre—and being open to new and different types of people, the exact opposites of the kind an Aquarius may have been associating with in the past, would be good ways to find love. It is not unusual for Aquarians to be brought together with a potential love interest through unusual circumstances, since the sign itself rules coincidences.

Finding That Special Someone

People do not usually have to make sweeping, radical changes in their lives to bring in the love that they desire, especially the kind of extreme changes that an Aquarian would be willing to make without a second's thought. For Aquarius, radical change is usually less complicated than for other signs, simply because Aquarians don't choose to do things according to plan. Aquarians don't question if a love interest comes into their life; they just accept it as a blessing from the universe.

First Dates

Because Aquarians are up for virtually anything at any time, a first date can be whatever they or their dates choose. Plans for a first date could range from activities as disparate as taking a ride on bumper cars, to an evening volunteering at a shelter or soup kitchen, to a night spent gambling at a private club. There really aren't any no-no's when it comes to taking out an Aquarius for the first time. Aquarians can enjoy themselves in any number of ways, so long as the person they are with is as open, accepting, and spontaneous as they are.

Aquarius in Love

Aquarians attract the opposite sex by their friendly, open manner, though they sometimes may try to seem glamorously aloof. Aquarians can be afraid of a deeply emotional involvement but genuinely want a real friendship with their loved ones. An Aquarian guards her independence and could even enjoy a living-apart relationship. A partner who makes too many demands, becomes jealous, or tries to put limitations on Aquarius' freedom is sure to be dropped quite suddenly.

Undying Love

Often, Aquarians don't get involved in a love relationship, believing that it will become the be-all and end-all to them. Alas, Aquarians may misread or even second-guess their own emotions. Once they are deeply in love, however, they understand that it was only fear that was holding them back. They may not commit in the typical or conventional way. They are not always comfortable showing the depth of their love through sentimental behavior, but they will profess it often with sincere words and kind deeds.

Expectations in Love

Aquarians expect their personal freedom of movement and action to be respected. They need total understanding and tolerance of their eccentricities. Aquarians are completely loyal and faithful to their partners. They expect their partners to enjoy frequent visits from a wide variety of friends from every walk of life.

Both people in any relationship must feel free and independent. This may sound like a contradiction in terms, but people in successful relationships can tell you that they have actually found the freedom to be themselves fully through their relationships. Being true to herself is a spiritual quest for an independent Aquarian thinker. If a partner can be supportive of that goal, he will improve his relationship with an Aquarius. Nothing is more enjoyable for an Aquarius than to be appreciated for who she really is.

An Aquarian's life is filled with unexpected events that cause her, eventually, to feel liberated. These events disrupt the status quo in her life and the lives of those she loves. Every relationship can change for the better. That is what makes her so attractive in the first place.

What Aquarians Look For

Aquarians do not look for someone who will support them in every way or someone they can support in the same manner. More than anything, they want an equal—a person who will walk beside them, rather than lead or follow. Aquarians don't necessarily look for a love interest who will agree with their rather radical opinions. They appreciate people who have strong convictions of their own and who follow their own paths. Aquarians know that the better the friendship is, the better the love relationship will be.

If Aquarians Only Knew...

If Aquarians only knew the deep love and affection their friends and others have for them, they would feel secure and not be worried about or take issue with emotional intimacy in their relationships. They would give themselves a chance to explore the ups and downs of emotional involvement without worrying that it would complicate life for them. Aquarians, once they open the floodgates, can come to terms with both past and present life events that have been awaiting resolution.

Marriage

Once Aquarius has settled into a marriage, he does not like the idea of divorce and often wants to remain friends with a past partner. An Aquarian's relationships would benefit from actions calculated to improve his marriage. Joining, supporting, and advising a group or organization dedicated to relationships might strengthen an existing relationship or bring a new one into his life.

It is important to keep any relationship new and exciting. If Aquarius has done that, then his relationship is stronger than ever and ready for any unexpected challenges that might arise. If Aquarius has allowed things to get stuck at the same level with no growth or change, then he must get to work fixing it or his relationship will be tested by one or both partners acting rebelliously, out-of-the blue challenges, or both.

Aquarius' Opposite Sign

Leo is the complementary opposite sign of Aquarius. Although relations between them can be difficult, Leo can show Aquarius how to make choices to please the self, rather than for an ideal. In this way, Aquarius can build emotional self-confidence. Also, the ease with which Leos handle their emotions can be a real eye-opener for Aquarians, who sometimes hide their true feelings under layers of logic and analytical assessments. In the same way, Aquarius can teach Leo self-control and intellectual discipline.

Pairing Up

In general, if people display the characteristics typical of their sign, intimate relationships between an Aquarius and another individual can be described as follows:

Aquarius with Aquarius:	Harmonious, but represents a meeting of minds, not souls
Aquarius with Pisces:	Harmonious, if Aquarius will allow Pisces to be nurturing
Aquarius with Aries:	Harmonious; this pair makes a good business and romantic partnership
Aquarius with Taurus:	Difficult, unless Taurus allows Aquarius the freedom she needs
Aquarius with Gemini:	Harmonious; a quirky and unique love affair with great conversations
Aquarius with Cancer:	Turbulent but exciting, with lots of sexual magnetism
Aquarius with Leo:	Difficult yet electric; a pair who fight in public, make up in private

Aquarius with Virgo:	Turbulent, since they have almost nothing in common but love
Aquarius with Libra:	Harmonious; a perfect pair: soul mates, lovers, and friends
Aquarius with Scorpio:	Difficult yet profound; a relationship arranged by destiny
Aquarius with Sagittarius:	Harmonious; completely in tune with each other's wants and needs
Aquarius with Capricorn:	Harmonious, with difficult patches; a karmic connection

If Things Don't Work Out

If Aquarius wants out and a partner doesn't take the hint, Aquarius is fully capable of doing something to make the partner end the relationship. If the situation is reversed and Aquarius is left in the lurch, there is sure to be a period of emotional mourning, but after that he is ready to move on. Aquarius has way of always looking at life and events from a logical perspective, even when it involves love.

Aquarius at Work

There is a tendency in just about every Aquarian to make work the center of her life. Her sense of dedication to what she does is considerable, and it can be difficult for even the most loving spouse or caring family member or friend to pry her away from it. But those who love Aquarius should understand that to expect anything but 100 percent total dedication from her is unrealistic.

As long as Aquarians feel that the work being done is important, they don't give a great deal of thought to where they stand in the overall chain of command. They can manage to show leadership without being the actual leader, and because they work well alone or with others, they rarely clash with those working above or below them.

They may not give the impression of great efficiency, but Aquarians have a unique ability to organize facts and relate them with amazing clarity. Their talent for communication puts them in a class by themselves, and because they have such dedication to what they are doing, they never leave a job undone.

Typical Occupations

Aquarius can benefit from an investigation, analysis, innovation, or original idea. Scientist, astrologer, singer, charity worker, inventor, archeologist, radiographer, engineer, and humanitarian aid worker are all good career choices for an Aquarius. Working for groups that have organized for a common goal is favored. Some examples are trade unions and associations, fraternal organizations, credit unions, Internet chat rooms and the like, political groups, and environmental causes.

Aquarians work best on group projects. They make excellent researchers and admirable scientists, especially astronomers and natural historians. They may lead the field in photography, computer technology, or electronics. Aviation is also a natural vocation for Aquarians.

Aquarians' progressive talents are expressed well in writing and in broadcast television or radio presenter or writer. In the theater, they make good character actors and are natural mimics. Many Aquarians make fine and progressive musicians. They make effective welfare workers or educators.

Behavior and Abilities at Work

In the workplace, the typical Aquarius:

* dislikes routine and decision making
* likes to solve problems
* enjoys variety
* prefers mental to physical work
* enjoys working with a group

* has a good reputation among peers
* likes to work on her own

Aquarius As Employer

A typical Aquarius boss:

* is quick thinking and a shrewd analyst
* is receptive to new ideas
* does not play favorites
* dislikes workplace cliques
* is full of surprising talents
* shows generosity to those doing special work
* gives employees fair compensation
* does not forgive lies or broken promises
* keeps promises

Aquarius As Employee

A typical Aquarius employee:

* is aloof but gets along with most types
* is good at conceptualizing possibilities
* comes up with innovative ideas
* brings a fresh approach to any task
* frequently changes her job
* has great creative and analytical skills
* has leadership potential

Aquarius As Coworker

The typical Aquarian is a loner, despite having a lot of workplace-based friendships. But he has the attributes of an Air sign—being able to get along with many different kinds of people without difficulty. Aquarius works well in groups, as team leader, or as a subordinate.

Details, Details

Aquarians don't think of themselves as detail-oriented people, and for the most part, they aren't. But that is mostly by choice. Actually, they have a fine mind for handling details, and they are particularly proficient at delegating detailed work to others, while still keeping an eye on all the areas and endeavors that comprise a project. Probably their best instinct for detailed work is being able to translate numbers and facts into concepts.

One reason Aquarians may not feel comfortable handling details is their tendency to be somewhat absentminded. Their answer to this problem is to be nearly obsessive about writing things down. By keeping copious lists of facts, dates, times, and names, they are better able to manage projects that call for these things to be remembered. In this way, though Aquarians may worry quite a lot about keeping all their facts straight, they are probably better prepared than most people to handle them.

Money

Any award or contest whose payout is stretched out into the future is appropriate for an Aquarius. Those with an astrological connection or something to do with numerology, the science of numbers, are also favored. Additionally, any games and prizes with a scientific, space, futuristic, or historic theme attract an Aquarian's interest.

If an Aquarian comes up with an idea that she thinks can be sold, she should pursue it. Patent attorneys and venture capitalists may be receptive, especially to ideas for making people's lives better and longer and businesses more productive.

Computers and electronics are also favored moneymakers for Aquarians. A futuristic technology could be easy for an Aquarian to understand and profit from. Good fortune is more likely to come to an Aquarius through friends than through other ways. They may bring good fortune in the form of a gift or helpful advice.

Aquarians have a love/hate relationship with money. They love it for the freedom it brings, but they hate the fact that they only have so much of it and are therefore restricted by it. Aquarians are drawn to charitable causes and are often the anonymous donors of substantial amounts.

At Home

Aquarians can get so comfortable in their own home and their own space that they don't want to leave, which is one of the reasons many Aquarians work from home. But whether they do or not, they are at ease with an unconventional household schedule.

Behavior and Abilities at Home

Aquarius typically:

* enjoys high-tech TVs and sound equipment
* lives in an unusually decorated space
* has a diverse group of houseguests
* fills her home with oddities
* eats strange mixtures of food and drink
* uses many tools, gizmos, and gear
* collects interesting photos and art
* takes unconventional vitamins and supplements

Leisure Interests

While a great many of Aquarius' interests are intellectual, they also love tinkering with things, using their inventive skills to fix, create, or supplement technical gadgets or useful implements. Aquarians often work on several hobbies or interests at the same time.

The typical Aquarius enjoys the following pastimes:

* radical politics
* music, rhythm, and singing
* science fiction
* controlled exercise
* writing his personal journal
* scientific or inventive hobbies
* theater, comedy, and home movies
* flying, gliding, and parachuting

Aquarian Likes

* fame or recognition
* learning about the world
* quiet time to think
* dreams and mystical experiences
* surprises and brilliant ideas
* the latest techno gadgets
* telling others what they think
* eccentric friends
* studying history
* travel to exotic places

Aquarian Dislikes

* too much emotion
* people who are boring
* being taken for granted
* having freedom curtailed
* any kind of rip-off
* false advertising

* making loans or borrowing
* conformity
* revealing her own motives
* the herd mentality

The Secret Side of Aquarius

Inside anyone who has strong Aquarian influences is a person who is extremely uncertain of his true identity. The Aquarius ego is the most precarious in the zodiac, because it is the sign of nonconformity. Intellectual genius, practical eccentricity, and mental oddity are all linked with Aquarius. The Aquarius personality has a powerful intellect. Putting this brainpower to good, practical use is the best way for Aquarius to build his ego.

Uranus

Uranus is the planet of eccentricity, genius, rebelliousness, revolution, and invention. It represents the forces in life that want to keep things new, exciting, and on the edge. It symbolizes the crisis of middle age that occurs at age forty, when people are tested to see whether they have made their lives a statement of their unique individuality. Uranus rules electricity and electrical devices such as computers, radios, and television sets, dynamite and all explosives, and especially futuristic devices. Uranus is the planet of crazy theories and science fiction that will one day be revealed as scientific fact.

Uranus is the planet of the unusual and the extreme. Recent satellite photos reveal that unlike any other planet, it has its north pole, not its equator, pointed at the Sun! Uranus rules ankles and wrists, and intuitive intellect. Uranus also rules science, invention, and discovery as well as the science of astrology itself.

Bringing Up a Young Aquarius

It is good to show Aquarian children how there is a bit of the genius or eccentric inside of them. It is also a good idea to expose them to humanitarian goals. More importantly, it is important to show them how humanitarian goals are reached by interacting with others. Teach them the value of looking at each situation as if seeing it for the first time.

Young Aquarius has an analytical, inquiring mind that is constantly processing information. She needs plenty of exposure to new ways of doing, making, and trying out inventions. A calm environment is essential to young Aquarius, because she is so sensitive to underlying tensions in the home. In practical terms, she needs to be taught simple methods for remembering things and for communicating her ideas to others.

Like any child, Aquarius needs love, especially in the form of respect, listening, appreciation, and friendship. Young Aquarius tends to act detached and dispassionate, sometimes finding close, intimate relationships difficult. She often looks more confident and acts older than she actually is, so parental encouragement and genuine interest in her ideas and needs should be expressed to reassure her.

The Aquarius Child

The typical Aquarius child:

- tends to be forgetful
- is sensitive and intuitive
- has unpredictable moods
- possesses amazing talents
- finds everything and everyone interesting
- is generous and kind to friends
- can have sudden outbursts of temper

- rebels against rules and regulations
- has lots of friends
- is very bright and grasps ideas quickly

Aquarius As a Parent

The typical Aquarius parent:

- makes rational judgments
- is energetic and intelligent
- endorses modern educational theories
- does not overdiscipline or inhibit
- is prepared to discuss any problem
- encourages independence of thought
- does not like convention or conformity
- is a devoted friend for life

Health

Aquarians have vast amounts of energy but often drive themselves into the ground, not knowing when they are tired. They have the habit of not listening to others' advice to slow down, and they can be rebellious patients who won't admit defeat. Aquarians need lots of fresh air, plenty of sleep, and regular exercise to stay healthy. Often, their work puts great demands on their eyesight and their time, but they should never miss an appointment at the optician's. They can have poor circulation, manifesting itself in leg and ankle problems, which are the body parts that Aquarius rules.

FAMOUS AQUARIANS

Jennifer Aniston

Mikhail Baryshnikov

Garth Brooks

Sheryl Crow

James Dean

Charles Dickens

Christian Dior

Thomas Edison

Mia Farrow

Clark Gable

Michael Jordan

Abraham Lincoln

Charles Lindbergh

Wolfgang Amadeus Mozart

Paul Newman

Yoko Ono

Lisa Marie Presley

Ronald Reagan

Christina Ricci

Franklin Delano Roosevelt

Babe Ruth

John Travolta

Lana Turner

Oprah Winfrey

Virginia Woolf

"We need not feel ashamed of flirting with the zodiac. The zodiac is well worth flirting with."

—D.H. LAWRENCE

PISCES
February 19–March 20

PISCES
February 19–March 20

Planet: Neptune
Element: Water
Quality: Mutable
Day: Thursday
Season: winter
Colors: lavender, sea green, aqua
Plants: wisteria, gardenia, lotus
Perfume: ylang-ylang
Gemstones: aquamarine, coral, mother-of-pearl, pearl
Metal: tin
Personal qualities: Empathetic, artistic, compassionate,
selfless, and psychically attuned

Keywords

We call the following words "keywords" because they can help you unlock
the core meaning of the astrological sign of Pisces. Each keyword represents
issues and ideas that are of supreme importance and prominence in the lives
of people born with Pisces as their Sun sign. You will usually find that every
Pisces embodies at least one of these keywords in the way he makes a living:

*sensitivity • spiritualism • receptivity • moodiness • vagueness
suffering in silence • otherworldliness • inspiration • faith
idealism • alternative medicine • fantasy • imagination*

---

dreams • confusion • illusion • sacrifice • surrender
martyrdom • escape • drug addiction and alcoholism
mind-body-spirit connection • spirit guides • intuition • ESP

Pisces' Symbolic Meaning

Pisces is the last sign of the zodiac. Because it is the last of the twelve signs, it contains a bit of all of them. If they take the time and investigate a little, people born under this sign often realize that they are literally picking up on the feelings of others. This explains why Pisces people are so easily able to understand how other people are feeling.

In fact, Pisceans are so sensitive to the feelings of others that it is not good for them to be near people who are angry, sad, or disturbed. If they are in conflict with themselves as the Piscean symbol suggests—two fish locked in tension, forever pulling each other in opposite directions—one side of this conflict can represent the personality whose inner self is always preparing to retreat from the world.

Pisces is associated with both empathy and telepathy. This natural ability to be invisibly connected to those around them and those around the world is both the blessing and the curse of all Pisceans. It enables them to feel exactly how to help those they care about, which is a Piscean specialty, but it is exhausting and hard on a Piscean person's emotions to have other people's lives intrude so on their own.

Pisces is one of the four Mutable Sun signs in astrology (the other three are Gemini, Virgo, and Sagittarius). Mutable signs are able to adapt and adjust. Pisces is also one of the three Water Sun signs in the zodiac (the other two are Scorpio and Cancer). Water signs value their emotions and their intuition.

When they turn their sensitivity to the real world, Pisceans have the capacity to make incredible amounts of money in business ventures. If you think that seems unlikely given Pisces' reputation for dreaminess and escapism, remember that as the last sign, Pisces contains a bit of all the other ones. Pisceans are most aware of both the things that unite us all and the immense differences between people. This is one of their great strengths, but if they let themselves be totally ruled by their emotions or let the sorrow of the human condition push them to escapist behavior, it can turn into a great weakness. When they learn to balance their innate intuitive skills with a logical approach that does not ignore what is real but unpleasant, they can accomplish great things.

Recognizing a Pisces

Pisces people have an air of mystery. Their eyes are very sensitive and caring, and they typically have a warm smile and the quality of empathy. There is a quietness in their manner. They are approachable, as though they truly understand human sorrows and failings. Although they may appear slender or have delicate features, they possess an inner strength that seems to radiate from the soul.

Pisces' Typical Behavior and Personality Traits

- has a warm, sympathetic heart
- is very romantic
- is rarely jealous, but gets hurt all the same
- often appears vague and dreamy
- protects her emotional vulnerability
- talks slowly and is knowledgeable on many subjects
- is subtle while appearing to be helpless or incapable
- is organized; manages the finances extremely well
- has few prejudices
- is emotionally involved
- is not ambitious for status, fame, or fortune
- cannot easily be fooled

* has few material needs, but needs her dreams
* does not try to dominate her partner in any way
* needs to belong to someone

What Makes a Pisces Tick?

The lesson for Pisces centers on why her life does not provide her with as many opportunities as she would like to use her unique sensitivity to others to gain the appreciation of those she would most like to help and associate with. People born under the sign Pisces want to learn how to get close enough to people to be of assistance to them without becoming over-whelmed by their needs and neediness. The more honest and honorable a Piscean is, the more she hesitates. Pisceans seem to fear that the world will expect more of them than they can give.

The Pisces Personality Expressed Positively

A Pisces who is empowered by the best characteristics of the sign is a source of help and inspiration both to himself and to others. The sensitivity of Pisceans is most useful when those born under this sign have a good sense of self and a lot of confidence. When they do, they are wonderful people to be around—full of joy, inspiration, and profound intuition.

On a Positive Note

Pisceans displaying the positive characteristics associated with their sign also tend to be:

* shy, gentle, and kind
* trusting and hospitable
* understanding of others
* romantic
* loving and caring
* mystical

- creative
- helpful to anyone in distress
- compassionate

The Pisces Personality Expressed Negatively

Pisceans who are unable to separate themselves from the drama and unhappiness in other people's lives display the negative characteristics of their sign. They often feel dragged down by problems around them yet are frustrated by their inability to do anything to make them better. Disappointed Pisceans may seek escape through drugs or alcohol, the effects of which make them more powerless.

Negative Traits

Pisceans displaying the negative characteristics associated with their sign also tend to be:

- dependent
- escapist, potentially losing touch with reality
- sensationalist
- depressive and self-pitying
- temperamental
- gullible and liable to give their all in a lost cause
- prone to blaming themselves
- too emotionally involved with the problems of others

Ask a Pisces If…

Ask a Pisces if you want to know the meaning of life. The Piscean is unlikely to put it in terms as broad as this, but he will, by some small act or utterance, help you to understand that it is through compassion, caring, and a spirit that is open to receive the love of others that true happiness exists. Pisceans are plugged in to the universe in a way that is otherworldly.

Pisces As Friends

Pisces are humorous and caring friends, even if there are long periods of time between get-togethers. In general, Pisces like friends who are useful and reassuring. In return, they give unprejudiced understanding and loyalty to their friends. Pisces are emotionally attached to their friends and rarely take notice if a friend is taking advantage of this involvement. Pisces can be a confusing person, so arrangements to meet with friends may be difficult to make.

Pisceans always think up something interesting to do and enjoy any kind of artistic venture. They can sometimes seem cool and offhand. This is usually temporary and due to a moment of insecurity. Pisces does not find it easy to conform; friends with conservative attitudes may find this a difficulty.

Looking for Love

The element of sacrifice does not fit easily with the standard view of courtship and romance. The exception to this occurs when a Pisces meets someone through her dedication to helping others. If both partners are on the helping end, this relationship would be more prone to lasting than if one partner was helping the other person. This would not be a relationship founded on mutual support, so it might need substantial reworking if the person receiving help no longer needed it. Sometimes, relationships last only as long as the problems being worked on exist.

If a Pisces does not have a relationship, the problem may be caused by his trying to escape reality in some way. Any dependence on drinking, drugs, cults, or even traditional religion will prevent him from being himself and seeing people for who they really are. Pisces should never give up his own beliefs and identity in a relationship where to get or keep his partner he has to deceive her, or himself.

The Piscean quest for romance is rooted in fantasy as much as reality. For other signs, this can be a mistake. But Pisces needs the illusion to keep the reality of love alive. If there is no fantasy, Pisces cannot fall in love in the first place. As long as Pisces' partner understands that it is up to her to help support the fantasy and, occasionally, make it come true, this way of looking at love works for Pisceans.

Finding That Special Someone

If a Pisces works in an artistic atmosphere, she will most certainly find a love interest there, or at a cultural happening. Otherwise, being involved in charitable causes will put Pisceans into contact with people who share their need to do good things for others.

First Dates

Pisceans enjoy the hearts-and-flowers routine, but only if it is sincere and not just an attempt to flatter their ego. Pisceans are more traditional than they realize. They take pleasure in simple dates like dinner and a movie or just a stroll while holding hands. They are not impressed by fancy surroundings or decor, and are as likely to enjoy a midnight burger at an all-night diner as a gourmet meal at one of the city's best eateries. Pisces believes that it is the company, not the surroundings, that makes the date special.

Pisces in Love

To Pisces, there is no difference between love, affection, and romance. A Pisces is romantic, is eager to please, and adapts to the demands of the relationship. A Pisces who feels unloved is an unhappy person to whom life seems very gray. Love revitalizes Pisceans. They can sometimes appear to be delicate, helpless, or vulnerable, but being loved enables Pisceans to cope very well with a range of difficulties, problems, and tragedies and allows their spiritual nature to blossom.

Undying Love

A Pisces sometimes stays in a relationship even when he is being deceived or treated badly. He must face the problem and take immediate steps to correct it. Pisces may sometimes leave a relationship for no clear reason. If the partner will not do what is necessary, then Pisces should do everything he can to get out of the situation. Forgiveness can occur at a distance, too.

Pisces will often show much sympathetic understanding and will try to retain a friendly relationship with the one he has left.

Expectations in Love

Pisces is the most romantic sign of the zodiac. Once in love, Pisceans are very caring, sensitive, and ready to sacrifice their own happiness for the sake of those they love. However, all too often, denial is used as a way of avoiding reality. Many people would rather convince themselves that they are in a fine relationship than admit their problems. Even the most spiritual and powerful force in the universe, forgiveness, may be being used as a disguise for denial and weakness. If alcohol, drugs, abuse, violence, or adultery is standing between a Pisces and the truly loving relationship that she dreams of, these dangerous and destructive forces cannot be denied or condoned.

What Pisceans Look For

Most people say that they are more interested in what's "inside" than in a love interest's appearance, but Pisceans really mean it, though it is probably truer to say that their love makes anyone beautiful or handsome. Pisceans look for someone whose life and spirit can be transformed by their love. They may even fall in love with a person who is very troubled, so that they can act as their spiritual rescuer or savior.

If Pisces Only Knew...

If Pisces only knew that they are capable of extraordinary strength and discipline, they would not worry about not measuring up to the challenges, both big and small, that come their way. At times, what they perceive to be a weakness is actually strength in the way that their great sensitivity allows them to deal with burdens that other, less-perceptive people cannot handle. Pisceans are accustomed to being treated by others as if they are emotionally fragile beings, and at times this causes them to have a less-than-stellar opinion of themselves, which is unfair.

Marriage

The married Pisces will bring great joy to the household with his wonderful imagination. Marriage gives male Pisces more self-assurance. The person who contemplates becoming the marriage partner of a typical Pisces must realize that Pisces will expect to be supported—emotionally or financially. Given this, the person who partners Pisces can expect loyalty and sensitive understanding in return.

Partners should be prepared to undertake the practical, administrative side of the marriage, leaving Piscean partners free to draw upon their artistic natures, and therefore exercise their creativity and understanding.

Pisces wants a marriage partner who supports and encourages her dreams in every respect. Pisces may sometimes appear to be a helpless, absentminded person but once she feels secure in the relationship, she feels free to believe in the beauty and spiritual goodness of their partnership.

Pisces' Opposite Sign

Detail-conscious Virgo is Pisces' complementary sign. Like Pisces, Virgo is compassionate and eager to be of service, but is more disciplined and can help Pisces understand how best to shoulder her responsibilities in the

---

world. Virgo can teach Pisces the value of self-discipline and how to become motivated. Pisces' gentleness has the power to make Virgo understand that sometimes criticism is just plain harping.

Pairing Up

In general, if people display the characteristics typical of their sign, intimate relationships between a Pisces and another individual can be described as follows:

Pisces with Pisces:	Harmonious; a truly romantic pairing with incredibly soulful results
Pisces with Aries:	Harmonious, though Aries will always want to take the lead
Pisces with Taurus:	Harmonious, creating a good balance between passion and domesticity
Pisces with Gemini:	Difficult, if Gemini can't appreciate Pisces' spiritual side
Pisces with Cancer:	Harmonious; a happily-ever-after relationship
Pisces with Leo:	Turbulent, yet with a karmic connection that just won't quit
Pisces with Virgo:	Difficult, but the partners are supportive of each other's needs
Pisces with Libra:	Turbulent, unless Pisces allows Libra to shine in the spotlight
Pisces with Scorpio:	Harmonious; deeply spiritual and incredibly passionate
Pisces with Sagittarius:	Difficult; an emotional roller coaster, but fun
Pisces with Capricorn:	Harmonious, so long as Capricorn learns to be tender
Pisces with Aquarius:	Harmonious, since personality differences can't spoil their love

If Things Don't Work Out

It can be very difficult for a Piscean to get out of an unhappy relationship. Even if there is no love left, Pisces is sure to continue to feel a sense of duty to his partner. It doesn't matter to Pisceans if there is clearly someone at fault in the breakup, because they will feel that it is at least partially their fault. Initially it isn't easy for them to move on after a breakup, but after a period that constitutes emotional mourning, they are ready to move forward with their life.

Pisces at Work

Pisceans can be very happy at work so long as they understand that they should not look to find all their contentment and satisfaction from doing a job. They don't always know that striking a balance is important in life, but they do notice it if there is something lacking in their existence as a result.

Even though Pisceans may be talented in their chosen field, it does not necessarily mean that the mantle of leadership comes easily to them. Actually, they may be uncomfortable with it, and so it can take a lot of talking by a person in authority whom they respect to make Pisceans realize their true potential. Pisceans may need to go through a period of adjustment as they grow in to their skills and leadership role.

There is a spiritual element to everything a Pisces dedicates his life to, and this can include work. When properly motivated, Pisceans can find great success as well as happiness resulting from their success. Once Pisces learns that being career oriented does not go hand-in-hand with materialism and greed, he is ready to welcome success as an option.

Typical Occupations

Because of their versatility, Pisces often follow several vocations during their lifetime. Working with large institutions such as the government, hospitals, the armed forces, major corporations, or charitable causes suits them. The intuitive and spiritual qualities of Pisceans can lead them into careers in religion and spirituality, or to service as mediums, mystics, and healers. Still others are creative cooks and chefs. They have a love of water and can be found in work that keeps them near the sea.

Pisces are sometimes better working by themselves than for someone else. Their kind and sympathetic natures equip them for careers in charity, in catering to the needy, as nurses, as social and health-care workers, or as veterinarians.

Pisces' creativity includes a natural ability to imitate or mirror people as well as empathize with them. These attributes make them wonderful character actors, and many Pisceans find great fulfillment onstage or in films. Pisces are effective in civil service, law enforcement, and the legal and judicial arena.

Behavior and Abilities at Work

In the workplace, the typical Pisces:

* does not like a strict schedule
* prefers to be behind the scenes
* enjoys work that stimulates creativity
* likes working alone or in a self-directed position
* needs flexibility and frequent change of routine

Pisces As Employer

A typical Pisces boss:

* serves people
* is a creative problem solver
* uses intuition to make decisions
* is a shrewd judge of character
* has a caring disposition

- may use drugs or alcohol
- is charitable and values kindness
- helps staff with personal problems
- may act tough to hide a sensitive nature

Pisces As Employee

A typical Pisces employee:

- is helpful and kind
- has an understanding of the human condition
- needs to exercise her creative imagination
- is sometimes untidy
- may be depressed or moody
- is very affected by negativity
- is a loyal worker when happy
- has good instincts about people

Pisces As Coworker

Pisceans enjoy being in a harmonious workplace and do their part to make the atmosphere pleasant. They have the ability to achieve an overview of any business situation, and their sensitivity enables them to know how others will feel and act. In business, Pisceans work best in creative positions and in public relations, but they may find it hard to do routine jobs or work in groups.

Details, Details

Pisces is something of a detail-challenged sign—at least this is the perception that many Pisceans have of themselves. They tend to feel that if they fail at the finer points of a project, they won't be able to handle the larger issues. But in point of fact that is not the case. Pisceans have the great gift of intuition, which helps them in all areas of life, but is predominantly helpful at work. This is because they do not always see themselves in the most favorable light in their work and may have to be convinced of their capabilities.

One way Pisceans are good at handling details is the manner in which they use them to illuminate a larger truth. Pisceans are so sensitive and intuitive that even the smallest matters can give them information that very few other people would be able to divine, or even notice at all. Also, although Pisceans may not "file" information in their memories very carefully, they have the ability to ransack their subconscious mind to call up important details when they need them.

Money

Money is a complicated issue for many Pisceans. They are not materialists in the true sense of the word, and on some level this can work against them. However, when they are in the mood to spend money on the nonessential pleasures of life, they are sometimes guilty of requiring immediate gratification. If they are not careful, this can lead to bad habits that have a negative effect on their life as well as their pocketbook.

Pisceans have an intuitive understanding about nonfinancial resources, and these they handle very well. Falling into this category are friendship, love, the goodwill of those who love them, and even favors that they can depend on the people they love to do, should they be needed. In this way they are extremely capable.

At Home

For a typical Piscean, home is a place where she needs to feel loved. Home can be a palace or a hovel, but it must contain people toward whom she is drawn emotionally and who love her. It is important for Pisces to feel safe and secure in her environment.

Behavior and Abilities at Home

Pisces typically:

- needs a private, personal space
- chooses good food and wine
- likes to escape to the bedroom
- enjoys exploring her imagination
- probably has no fixed routine
- is likely to be untidy
- needs to be surrounded by art and soothing design
- should keep a clock in every room

Leisure Interests

Pisceans love artistic pursuits and anything that has an element of mystery, fantasy, and imagination. Dangerous sports, such as skydiving or car racing, can also appeal to Pisceans because they have an unerring instinct in such situations. The Piscean love of spirituality is enhanced by nature-related activities such as gardening and taking long walks.

The typical Piscean enjoys the following pastimes:

- theater and films
- stories about witches, monsters, and creatures
- gentle foot massages
- noncompetitive sports
- watercolor classes
- scented bubble baths

Piscean Likes

- romantic places
- candles and incense

- people who need their help
- sleeping and dreaming
- being loved
- reading and writing poetry
- yoga and meditation
- shoes
- mystical gifts and psychics
- soft background music

Piscean Dislikes

- harsh, bright lighting
- being sleep deprived
- people knowing too much about them
- stiff or tight clothing
- noisy, crowded places
- dirty jokes
- being told to get a grip on things
- ugly places
- insensitive people
- skeptical attitudes

The Secret Side of Pisces

Sometimes Pisceans desire to escape from experiencing both their own emotions and the emotions of those around them. No one is better than those born under this sign at creating their own fantasy world, through writing and the visual arts, mood-altering substances, or earning enough money to make their world as isolated and comfortable as possible. They get into trouble when they use drugs, alcohol, sex, gambling, religious zealousness, and other escape devices that overwhelm their common sense and block out the real world.

Neptune

Neptune is the planet of transcendent beauty and inspiration. It rules theories about dimensions beyond this one, faith, and the belief in things that cannot be seen, the power of prayer, and the afterlife. When the beauty and idealization of Neptune become clouded by fear, the tendency to want to escape can be as overwhelming as the ocean's currents. This is why Neptune is also associated with drugs, alcohol, and other escapist behavior. It also rules psychic phenomena, when people may actually visit the realms of spiritual power beyond the earthly one. This is the world of intuition, mental telepathy, and extrasensory perception of all kinds.

Neptune rules the feet, and those who learn about the science of reflexology will discover that there are points in the feet that connect to all the other parts of the body.

Bringing Up a Young Pisces

Piscean children absorb information and ideas like a sponge. They should be taught to sort their ideas and to distinguish between what is reality and what is fantasy.

Young Pisceans tend to be vulnerable to friends who might deceive them. Because of their compassionate, passive, and sweet natures, Piscean children may sometimes be the victims of bullies, so it would be useful to teach them strategies for dealing with such situations. An understanding of human nature and some simple, clear rules help young Pisces to avoid those pitfalls—while still developing their valuable traits of love and understanding.

Emotional connections with people are absolutely essential to Piscean happiness. The young Piscean is less concerned with places or things, although they often seek attachments to animals. Consequently, a Pisces child should be helped to believe in herself and prevented from becoming too clingy.

At school, young Pisces usually do not take leadership positions—they prefer to avoid the limelight. However, Piscean children are the source of wonderful ideas for art, play, and adventure. Because they have highly attuned artistic impulses, they should be encouraged to find a channel for their abilities. However, it is a mistake to push them, since their delicate spirit needs to be fostered, not forced.

The Pisces Child

The typical Pisces child:

* loves the world of make-believe
* goes his own way
* has an active imagination
* believes in fairies and angels
* rarely loses his temper
* has a sweet and engaging smile
* has secret conversations with spirits
* is artistically gifted
* loves animals
* looks like something is wrong when lost in thought
* knows how others are feeling
* blurts out things she has no way of knowing—psychic!
* can easily have his feelings hurt
* wants to help those in need
* needs help standing up to bullies

Pisces As a Parent

The typical Pisces parent:

* encourages the creativity of children
* tends to spoil and overprotect

- may forgive rather than discipline
- listens with understanding
- encourages intuitive development
- may have to try to be punctual
- rarely curses or uses harsh language
- may tend to have an unusual set of rules
- shares fairy tales and magical tales

Health

Typical Pisceans are healthy people as long as they are loved. Unhappy Pisceans are vulnerable to alcohol, drugs, or other ways of escaping reality, which is not good for their mental and physical health.

Pisceans can worry, and tend to develop insomnia. If they do relaxing forms of exercise or meditation, they can stay positive. The constant effort of avoiding negativity is the cause of much distress to many Pisceans, who are so intuitive, they often know when someone else is ill and can feel their pain.

Pisceans also need to take care of their feet, which is the part of the body that Pisces rules. They should always wear comfortable shoes.

FAMOUS PISCEANS

Drew Barrymore

Harry Belafonte

Alexander Graham Bell

Johnny Cash

Edgar Cayce

Frederic Chopin

Kurt Cobain

Albert Einstein

Jackie Gleason

Kelsey Grammer

Spike Lee

Jerry Lewis

Eva Longoria

Liza Minnelli

Anaïs Nin

Chuck Norris

Sidney Poitier

Lou Reed

Auguste Renoir

John Steinbeck

Sharon Stone

Elizabeth Taylor

George Washington

Vanessa Williams

Bruce Willis

"I will look on the stars and look on thee and
read the page of thy destiny."

—LETITIA ELIZABETH LANDON

✳ *About the Authors* ✳

Monte Farber and Amy Zerner

Internationally known self-help author Monte Farber's inspiring guidance and empathic insights impact everyone he encounters. Amy Zerner's exquisite, one-of-a-kind spiritual couture creations and collaged fabric paintings exude her profound intuition and deep connection with archetypal stories and healing energies. For more than thirty years they've combined their deep love for each other with the work of inner exploration and self-discovery to build The Enchanted World of Amy Zerner and Monte Farber: books, card decks, and oracles that have helped millions answer questions, find deeper meaning, and follow their own spiritual paths.

Together they've made their love for each other a work of art and their art the work of their lives. Their best-selling titles include *The Chakra Meditation Kit, The Tarot Discovery Kit, Karma Cards, The Enchanted Spellboard, Secrets of the Fortune Bell, Little Reminders: Love & Relationships, Little Reminders:*

The Law of Attraction, Goddess, Guide Me!, The Enchanted Tarot, The Instant Tarot Reader, The Psychic Circle, Wish Upon a Star Cosmic Fortune-Telling Kit, The Truth Fairy, Tarot Secrets, The Mystic Messenger, Healing Crystals, The Healing Deck, Quantum Affirmations, and *Buddha Beads.*

Websites: www.TheEnchantedWorld.com
www.AmyZerner.com
www.MonteFarber.com

Twitter: @AmyZerner & @askMonte
Facebook: The Enchanted World

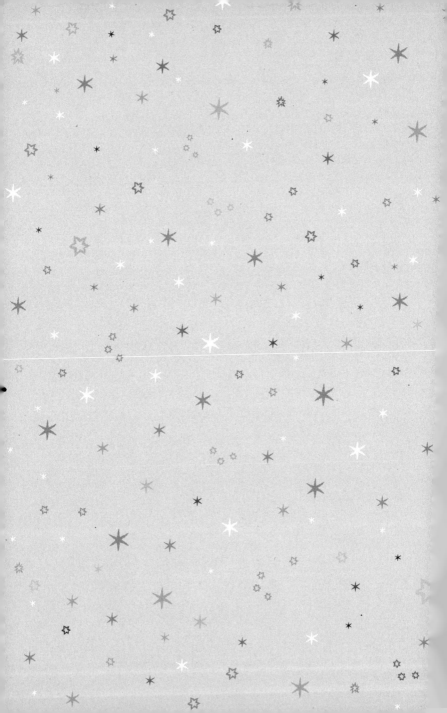